Talk and Write!

*A **Photocopyable** Collection of*
Writing Activities

Writing to Remember
Writing with the Five Senses
Writing Around the Holidays
Writing with Imagination
Writing Activities for Pairs and Groups
Writing Poetry

Janet Morey
Gail Schafers

PRO LINGUA ASSOCIATES

Pro Lingua Associates, Publishers
P.O. Box 1348
Brattleboro, Vermont 05302-1348 USA
Office: 802 257 7779
Orders: 800 366 4775
E-mail: orders@ProLinguaAssociates.com
SAN: 216-0579

Webstore: www.ProLinguaAssociates.com

At *Pro Lingua*
our objective is to foster an approach
to learning and teaching that we call
interplay, the *inter*action of language
learners and teachers with their materials,
with the language and culture,
and with each other in active, creative,
and productive *play*.

Copyright © 2011 by Janet Morey and Gail Schafers

Some activities are based on *Write for You*, copyright © 2001 by the authors.
Copyright information on material used in this book with permission is given on page vi.

ISBN 13: 978-0-86647-320-0; 10: 0-86647-320-3

Illustration credits: Photos on pages 15, 17, 33, and 83 are by Janet Morey. The following illustrations are from the Dreamstime. com Agency – x © Konstantin Sutyagin; 7 © Mehmet Dilsiz; 27 © Manina; 31 © Radu Razvan Gheorghe; 39 © Tatyana Chernyak, © Monkey Business Images, © Svitlana, © Jonald John Morales; 41 © Silberschuh9875; 45 © Jonathan Ross; 53 © Jinyoung Lee; 54 © Teslenko Petro; 57 © Arenacreative; 59 © Nob50; 61 © Lokinthru; 63 © Ronnie Phipps; 65 © Tatjana Grinberg; 66 © Jill Battaglia; 73 © Madartists; 75 © Stephen Coburn; 80 © Plamen Petro; 87 © Thomas Popelka; 91 © Fancyfocus; 97 © Thomas Perkins; 105 © Bert Folsom; 107 © Monkey Business Images; 109 © Martin Muránsky; 110 © Mamahoohooba; 123 © Raphotography; 128 © Cedric Carter; 131 © Anatoliy Samara; 137 © Suzanne Tucker; 139 © Mircea Costina, © Okea; 141 © Michelle Millman; 142 © Rmarion. *The Child's Bath* by Mary Cassatt on page 5 is used by courtesy of the Robert Waller Fund and the Mr. and Mrs. M.A. Ryerson Collection (connected with the Art Institute of Chicago). The rest of the artwork in this book was collected by the authors from various free clipart collections.

This book was designed by Arthur A. Burrows based on the design of the authors. It was set in graceful Adobe Garamond, designed by Robert Slimbach (1956-) in 1989. This font is based on 16th-Century French roman faces by Claude Garamond (1490-1561) and italics by his colleague Robert Granjon (1513-1590). The contrasting sans-serif typeface used for display and some quoted text is Trebuchet, developed in 1996 for Microsoft by Vincent Connare; he named it for a mediaeval siege engine, because he hoped it would catapult words and ideas across the internet. Its letter forms are elegant. The book was printed and bound by Victor Graphics of Baltimore, Maryland.

Printed in the United States of America
First printing 2011. 2000 copies in print.

Contents

Introduction: How to Use This Book ♦ viii

I. Writing to Remember ♦ 1

   1 Childhood Memories ♦ 2
   2 Mother ♦ 4
   3 Father ♦ 6
   4 What's Your Name? ♦ 8
   5 My First Day of School ♦ 10
   6 Teacher ♦ 12
   7 Best Friend ♦ 14
   8 First Love ♦ 16
   9 Cat, Dog, Parrot? ♦ 18
  10 Happiness ♦ 20
  11 Influences: People in Our Lives ♦ 22
  12 Memories in Small Bags ♦ 24
  13 Reflections on Water ♦ 26
  14 The Character Sketch ♦ 28
  15 Favorite Place ♦ 30
  16 Take Your Reader Shopping ♦ 32
  17 The Gift ♦ 34
  18 Mementos ♦ 36
  19 Your City or Town: A Detail in Focus ♦ 38
  20 Something from Home ♦ 40
  21 Changes ♦ 42
  22 Strange Encounters of a New Kind ♦ 44
  23 Conversation – A Lost Art? ♦ 46
  24 Rain ♦ 48
  25 Snow ♦ 50
  26 Choose Your Season ♦ 52

II. Writing with the Five Senses ♦ 55

   1 Are You Listening? ♦ 56
   2 Smell and Memory ♦ 58
   3 Touch ♦ 60
   4 Spring's Here! ♦ 62
   5 Chocolate Chip Cookie Day ♦ 64

Contents, continued

III. Writing Around the Holidays ♦ 67

1 Writing from the Heart ♦ 68
2 Heroes in History ♦ 70
3 St. Patrick's Day ♦ 72
4 BOO! ♦ 74
5 Ghost Stories ♦ 76
6 Voyages and Thanksgiving ♦ 78

IV. Writing with the Imagination ♦ 81

1 Finding Beauty in the Ordinary ♦ 82
2 An Imaginary Trip to an Art Museum ♦ 84
3 Drawing Into Writing ♦ 86
4 What Am I? ♦ 88
5 I Am A… ♦ 90
6 Folktales and Storytelling ♦ 92
7 One More Frog and Toad ♦ 94
8 Make a PB and J ♦ 96
9 Queen and King for a Day ♦ 98
10 Tick, Tock, I'm a Clock ♦ 100
11 Go Ahead, Exaggerate! ♦ 102
12 Shoes ♦ 104
13 Attitude Through Adjectives ♦ 106
14 An Autumn Leaf ♦ 108

V. Writing Activities for Pairs and Groups ♦ 111

1 The Personal Interview ♦ 112
2 Who Are They? What Do They Do? ♦ 114
3 What Happens Next? ♦ 116
4 Story from a Wordless Picture Book ♦ 118
5 Love Story ♦ 120
6 Writing as a Process ♦ 122
7 Writing a Thank-You Note ♦ 124
8 Keep Your Reader at the End of Your Pencil ♦ 126

Contents, continued

VI. **Writing Poetry** ♦ 129

   1 A First Look at Poetry ♦ 130
   2 What's Hanging on My Clothesline? ♦ 132
   3 Another Look at Poetry ♦ 134
   4 Poetry and Rhyme ♦ 136
   5 Color Your Poem ♦ 138
   6 Put Yourself in Poetry ♦ 140

Appendix: Handouts for III. Writing Around the Holidays ♦ 142

Writing from the Heart (Valentine's Day) ♦ 144
Heroes in History ♦ 145
St. Patrick's Day ♦ 146
Halloween ♦ 147
Voyages and Thanksgiving ♦ 148

Skills Index ♦ 149

Adjectives
Brainstorming
Comparison and Contrast
Dialogue
Hyperbole
Hyphenated Modifiers
Imagery
Mood
Narrowing Focus
Poetry
Point of View/Personification
Sensory Writing
Similes and Metaphors
Speed Writing
Transitions
Writing in the Descriptive
Writing in the Expository
Writing in the Narrative

Dedication

Dedicated to all our students who over the years inspired us to write this book

Acknowledgements

Student writing samples for this publication came from new writers at Fontbonne University, St. Louis Community College, and the Parkway Adult Education and Literacy Program.

Literary snippets were gathered from twenty-six authors, ranging from Charles Dickens to J. K. Rowling to John Steinbeck to Alexander McCall Smith.

We wish to thank the Robert Waller Fund and the Mr. and Mrs. M. A. Ryerson Collection (connected with the Art Institute of Chicago) for permitting us to use the Mary Cassatt print, *The Child's Bath*, in the *Mother* unit.

Special appreciation goes to Arthur A. Burrows and his lovely wife, Elise, of Pro Lingua Associates, a highly respected Vermont publishing house of excellent educational materials. They have labored meticulously to help us bring forth *Talk and Write!* Our thanks, too, to Raymond C. Clark, who skillfully edited our first book and made many helpful suggestions for the development of this one. Their long experience and expertise have been a tremendous support to us. We are most thankful to them.

Credits ♦ *Literary Snippets Used*

(in order of appearance in the book)

♦ *Memoirs of a Geisha.* © Arthur Golden, Alfred A. Knopf, Inc., New York, New York. 1997
♦ *David Copperfield.* © Charles Dickens, Oxford University Press, Inc., United Kingdom of Great Britain and Northern Ireland. 1981
♦ *Great Expectations.* © Charles Dickens, Palgrave McMillan, United Kingdom of Great Britain and Northern Ireland. 1998
♦ *"Antonio's First Day of School"* from *Bless Me, Ultima.* © Rudolfo A. Anaya, TQS Publications, Eclectic Chicano Literature, Oakland, California. 1976
♦ *Harry Potter and the Sorcerer's Stone.* © J. K. Rowling, Bloomsbury, United Kingdom. 1997, Scholastic, New York, New York. 1998
♦ *The House at Pooh Corner.* © A.A. Milne, Penguin USA, New York, New York, 1961
♦ *"All I Ask Of You"* from *Phantom of the Opera.* © Andrew Lloyd Webber, Omnibus Press, United Kingdom of Great Britain and Northern Ireland. 1987
♦ *The Cat Who Walked Across France.* © Kate Banks, Frances Foster Books/Farrar, Straus and Giroux, Atlanta, Georgia. 2004
♦ *Of Mice and Men.* © John Steinbeck, Bantam Books, New York, New York. 1983
♦ *The House on Mango Street.* © Sandra Cisneros, Random House, Inc., New York, New York. 1994
♦ *the bracelet.* © Yoshiko Uchida, Philomel Books, New York, New York. 1993
♦ *"The Oyster"* from *Mooltiki: Stories and Poems from India.* © Rumer Godden, Curtis Brown Ltd, London, England. 1957
♦ *The No. 1 Ladies Detective Agency.* © Alexander McCall Smith, Anchor Books (Random House), New York, New York. 2002
♦ *The Story of Edgar Sawtelle.* © David Wroblewski, Bond Street Books (Doubleday Canada), Toronto, Ontario, Canada. 2008
♦ *The Yearling.* © Marjorie Kinnan Rawlings, Simon & Schuster Adult, New York, New York, 1985
♦ *Snow Falling on Cedars.* © David Guterson, Gale Group, Belmont, California. 1996
♦ *Thunder Cake.* © Patricia Polacco, Philomel Books, New York, New York. 1990
♦ *Rascal.* © Sterling North, Penguin USA, New York, New York. 1984
♦ *Old Devil Wind.* © Bill Martin, Jr., Harcourt Brace & Company, New York, New York. 1993
♦ *"Leaf"* from *Papa, You're Crazy.* © William Saroyan, Little, Brown and Company, Boston, Massachusetts. 1957
♦ *I Walk at Night.* © Lois Duncan, Penguin USA, New York, New York. 2000
♦ *Frog and Toad Are Friends.* © Arnold Lobel, HarperCollins Publishers, New York, New York. 1970
♦ *John Henry.* © Julius Lester, Penguin USA Juvenile, New York, New York. 1994
♦ *How Does the Wind Walk?* © Nancy White Carlstrom, Macmillan Publishing Company, New York, New York. 1993

A Note from the Authors

While team-teaching an ESL class of forty at a large adult education facility a few years ago, we searched for a writing textbook without finding one we loved. We turned to our colleagues. Several told us they kept writing instruction to a minimum, as they considered grammar, speaking, and listening much more important.

With no writing manual in hand, and little help from fellow teachers initially, we made up some lesson plans, tested them in our class, and retained the best ones. Our lessons worked, to spirited enthusiasm from our students and better and better results. Students became excited about writing. "I hated writing in my first language," remarked one, "but I love writing in English!" "I think what I just wrote is really *good!* Can I read it to the class?" asked another. More and more strategies came to us, and one day, we looked at each other and said, "Wouldn't it be fun to write a book?" We were on our way!

We moved on to separate schools, one of us to direct the ESL program at a local university, the other to become a community college instructor. At both locations, we found writing emphasized throughout the curriculum. We kept in close touch with each other over the years, meeting regularly to update, revise, and add freshness to meet current needs.

We are happy now to share these lessons with you. The units are autonomous and may be used in any order. Each one takes approximately an hour and a quarter of class time. In addition, the assignments may be expanded to cover several class periods, which allows time for editing and revision.

At the beginning of each term, we remind our students that they bring their backgrounds, values, and experiences into everything they write. Since these components are theirs alone, they will express themselves differently from each of their classmates. Their writing will become as individual as their fingerprints. We encourage them to "play with words" until they choose the best ones for their purposes. Mark Twain said, "The difference between the right word and the almost right word is the difference between lightning and the lightning bug." Writing is an adventure!

Janet Morey and Gail Schafers

Introduction
How to Use This Book

This book is designed to help native or non-native speakers of English develop their writing skills and enjoy the process of writing. The activities are appropriate for learners in middle school, high school, communty college, college preparation, and adult education courses. With minor adjustments, they also can be used with elementary school students. Non-native learners from the intermediate to the advanced proficiency levels and even those in TOEFL preparation courses find the structured development activities useful; some units can be adapted for high-beginner learners.

Students, particularly those learning English, frequently find writing the most difficult of the language skills to master. Good writing demands correct grammar usage and sentence structure; accurate spelling; varied, original vocabulary; and careful organization. Using this teacher-friendly material, students will learn to strengthen writing beyond these basics by focusing on such stylistic or artistic elements as imagery, mood, simile and metaphor, hyperbole, personification and point-of-view, hyphenated modifiers, dialogue, description, and narrative.

These activities have been designed to engage the students personally and creatively, instilling in them a love of writing as they learn to take pride in expressing themselves "on paper." As the authors see it, while students are developing specific skills (see the skill index at the back of the book), they should also have fun. We encourage them to "play with words," to enjoy the process, the adventure of writing and writing well.

Each unit has two pages, a teacher's page and a ***photocopyable*** student handout. The teacher's page first states the objective of the exercise. When materials are needed for the activity, they are listed. And then there is a step-by-step explanation of what the teacher and the students will do. Typically these steps begin with a teacher-led discussion explaining the activity and its purpose. This is followed by pairwork or small-group discussion. Then the handout is given to the students, and they follow the instructions given there.

There are six sections of the book. The first prompts learners to draw on personal memories, to share them in conversation, and then to write about them. The second section has the learners write descriptively using the senses of hearing, smell, touch, sight, and taste.

In the third section, the authors ask the learners to write creatively about emotions, heroes, cultural celebrations, the fun of telling spooky stories, and the adventure of moving across cultures, of starting over. In this section, the teacher may want to keep the focus primarily on the learners' own experience or to introduce cultural material about five popular American holidays, Valentine's Day, Presidents' Day, St. Patrick's Day, Halloween, and Thanksgiving. An optional special reading on each holiday is appended starting on page 142.

In the fourth section of the book, the learners use their imaginations to write about a variety of fanciful "what-if" situations. In the fifth, they experiment with storytelling of various kinds, working in pairs and small groups. And in the sixth, learners are encouraged to play with the language, writing some simple poems.

This book is a ***photocopyable*** teacher's resource. It is structured so that it can be used as the basis for a writing course, following the sequence in which the units are presented. However, many teachers will want to pick and choose, selecting activities that will fit their students' particular needs and interests or to supplement a prescribed curriculum. Many of the skills practiced are stipulated in state assessment guidelines around the United States.

Janet Morey and Gail Schafers have adapted some of these materials from their 2001 book, *Write for You*. However, the format and process of these activities have been completely revised, and all the activities have been drawn from the authors' own classroom experience and tested with a variety of classes both by colleagues and themselves. This is a rich resource for any writing teacher, and we hope that you will enjoy turning your students on to the art and pleasure of writing as much as the authors have.

Pro Lingua Associates

I. Writing to Remember

Unit 1 ♦ Childhood Memories
teacher's page

Objective: Students will think back on their childhood and write a narrative essay.

Steps:

1. Tell students that you are going to talk about some of the things you remember from your childhood. Start with the expression, "I remember..." and talk about some activity that you remember. Do this five times.

2. Pair students. Instruct them to do the same, using the "I remember..." format. Partners should take turns making statements.

3. After 15 minutes, stop the students. Pass out the handout, and have students do the writing assignment.

Childhood Memories
student handout

"When I was a child, I used to talk as a child, think as a child, reason as a child; when I became a man, I put aside childish things."

I Corinthians 13:11

With your partner, you talked about some of the things you remember from your childhood. Now think back on one memory, and write about it.

Unit 2 ♦ Mother
teacher's page

Objective: After reminiscing about their mothers, students will each write about their mother, or about a mother figure important to them.

Materials: Copies of 3-4 Mary Cassatt paintings, found under Google, *Mary Cassatt – The Complete Works.* Choose only those that portray mothers and children, such as *The Child's Bath,* shown on the student handout. If this is not possible, either find some prints of Cassatt paintings in the library or collect some other pictures of mothers with their children.

Steps:

1.   Show the Cassatts you have brought. Display them around the room, or show them on a visual presenter. Can the students guess what they will be writing about for this lesson? (When they guess mothers, congratulate them on their smartness!)

2.   *(Optional)* Tell the class briefly about Cassatt's life (see the box below), or simply talk about the paintings. What do they show? (The close relationship between mothers and children or simple activities between mothers and children.) Have students come up with "mother" adjectives, and put these on the board.

3.   Pair the students to describe their mothers (or, if anyone prefers, a "mother" who is important to them). Next they should tell of an important lesson their mother taught them or an experience they enjoyed together.

4.   Go to the student handout to follow the directions there.

Mary Cassatt (1844-1926)

Mary Cassatt was probably the most famous American woman painter. People remember her most for her paintings of the private lives of women, especially the tender relationship between mothers and children.

Cassatt was born in Pittsburgh, Pennsylvania. Her father did not want her to become an artist, and he refused to pay for her art supplies. It was not considered proper for women to be painters at that time. However, she had a passion for art, and she was determined to paint professionally. She moved to Paris and spent most of her life in France. Eventually she was invited to join the Impressionist group of artists.

Mary Cassatt became much more well-known in Europe than in her own country. She died in 1926.

Mother

My Mother

I closed my eyes. I flew back in time. My mother was sitting by the window. She had pushed the curtain away. Her face was bright because of the light coming from the window. It was four in the afternoon.

She was quiet as always. I was watching her; how beautiful she was! How much I wanted to touch her! I wanted to sit there and smell her hair. I wanted to put my head on her shoulder and close my eyes. I wanted her to caress me. That always made me relaxed.

I was listening to the song that her knitting needles were making. How peaceful that was, and how much I loved that sound! I knew that I had to go, back to the time I was coming from. I wasn't a child anymore. I wasn't in the same house anymore. Maybe I wasn't the same person anymore.

However, I won't ever forget those memories. Never.

Anonymous, College ESL student

Does the piece above remind you of your own mother? Why, or why not?

For this lesson, you will write about your mother (or, if you prefer, someone who was like a mother to you: a grandmother, relative, friend, teacher). First, describe her.

Then, relate an unforgettable lesson she taught you, or a compelling experience you shared.

Unit 3 ♦ Father
teacher's page

Objective: Students will write a descriptive essay about their father, a father figure in their lives, or the ideal father.

Materials: *(Optional)* pictures of your father or father figure

Steps:

1. Pass around pictures of your father to the class, and ask the students if they can guess who this person is. Identify the person, and then talk about him. You can give a physical description, talk about your memories of him, describe his life before you were a part of it, *etc.*

2. Write the word "father" on the board. Ask students to add any variants they may have heard: daddy, dad, pop, papa, *etc.*

3. Ask the class for the word – and variants – they use in their language for father.

4. Pair the students and have them talk about their own fathers, a father figure in their lives, or an "ideal" father.

5. Allow about 15 minutes for discussion, and then distribute the student handout.

Father

We have been talking about fathers in class. Here is an example of a well-written description of a father:

> "...my father was more at ease on the sea than anywhere else, and never left it far behind him. He smelled like the sea even after he had bathed. When he wasn't fishing, he sat on the floor in our dark front room mending a fishing net. And if a fishing net had been a sleeping creature, he wouldn't even have awakened it, at the speed he worked. He did everything this slowly... One day I asked him, 'Daddy, why are you so old?' He hoisted up his eyebrows at this, so that they formed little sagging umbrellas under his eyes. And he let out a long breath, and shook his head and said, 'I don't know.'"
>
> From *Memoirs of a Geisha* by Arthur Golden

Now it is time for you to write about your father, a father figure in your life, or the ideal father. To make your composition interesting, include a description of this person's physical appearance. Give details about him as Arthur Golden did in the passage above, so that he will seem real to the reader.

Unit 4 ◆ What's Your Name?
teacher's page

Objective: After discussing the significance of names, students will write about the cultural origins and meanings of their first names.

Steps:

1. Begin this lesson by asking students why they think that people's names are important.

2. Invite your class to tell something interesting about names in their countries. (For instance, in Pakistan some fathers and sons all have the same first names, such as Mirza. Middle names provide individuality. In Togo, parents name their children after the weekday of their birth.)

3. Parents think long and hard about naming children. Writers have fun naming characters. Distribute the handout; read it together.

4. Pair the students. They will follow the guidelines at the bottom of the handout. After ten or fifteen minutes, go around the class, asking students to tell one fact about their **partners'** first names. Students will then write on their own first name.

What's Your Name?
student handout

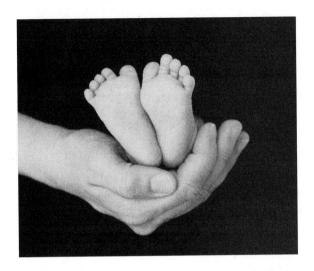

name, n. a word or set of words by which someone is known, addressed, or referred to.

name, v. give a name to; identify...

from *Oxford English Dictionary*

Look at two names created by Charles Dickens, a well-known British author:

> "Uriah Heep is seated on a high stool in Wickfield's office, thoughtfully cracking his knuckles as David comes in."
> from *David Copperfield*
>
> "Uncle Pumblechook was a large, hard-breathing, middle-aged, slow man, with a mouth like a fish, dull staring eyes, and sandy hair standing upright on his head."
> From *Great Expectations*

Discuss the following ideas with your partner. You will tell about your **first** name.

- ☞ Who named you? Parents? Grandparents?
- ☞ Does your first name have special meaning?
- ☞ Do you like your first name? If you don't like it and could select a different name, what would you choose?

Now, using these ideas, write about your **first name**.

Unit 5 ♦ My First Day of School
teacher's page

Objective: Drawing on their experience, students will write a narrative essay.

Procedure:

1. Tell the students that they are going to write about a past experience: their first day of school.

2. Divide the students into pairs. Tell them to think back to when they were children and the first day they went to school: who took them to school, what happened, what they remember about their teacher, what they remember about the place, and how they felt. If they can't remember the first day, tell them to think about their first memories of school. Allow them approximately 10-15 minutes to share.

3. The next topic they will discuss will be their first day in this school: what happened, what they remember about that first day, and how they felt. Allow another 10-15 minutes for discussion.

4. Distribute the handout. After reading it, the students will do the writing assignment.

My First Day of School
s t u d e n t   h a n d o u t

Below is a quotation from *Antonio's First Day of School* by Rudolfo Anaya.

> On the first day of school I awoke with a sick feeling in my stomach. It did not hurt; it just made me feel weak. The sun did not sing as it came over the hill... For the first time I would be away from the protection of my mother. I was excited and sad about it.

Notice that Rudolfo Anaya describes feeling both "excited and sad" about going to school. Were your feelings on your first day of school as a child similar to or different from his? Was the way you felt on your first day of school here different from the way you felt when you were a child? Were there any similarities?

Write a composition describing your first day of school. You can choose to write about:

♦ Your first day of school as a child
♦ Your first day of school here
♦ A comparison of the two "first days"

Objective: Students will recall a past teacher and bring that person to life on paper. In addition, they will add "hyphenated modifiers" to their writing skills.

Steps:

1. Ask the students to visualize a past teacher. This person might be their best or worst teacher. They can choose any teacher they remember. Give them some quiet moments to do this.

2. Next, request that the students jot down words (not complete sentences) about the teacher onto scrap paper. (This is called brainstorming, a well-recognized pre-writing technique.) Students will share these with a partner.

3. Then, teach the class about hyphenated modifiers, words that are fun to work with and that add interest to description. Compose a handout from the list below, or choose several to write on the board. See if the students can come up with more.

4. Distribute the student handout. Students will follow directions at the bottom.

Physical characteristics	*Non-physical characteristics*
heavy-set	soft-spoken, loud-mouthed
well-built	sad-looking, happy-looking
pear-shaped	mild-mannered
frail-looking	bad-mannered
delicate-looking	well-mannered
big-boned	quick-witted
bow-legged	hot-headed
blue-eyed, brown-eyed	level-headed
pale-faced	strong-willed
rosy-cheeked	thin-skinned
dark-haired	even-tempered
white-haired, gray-haired	self-confident
fair-skinned, dark-skinned	self-conscious
round-shouldered	thirty-year-old
stoop-shouldered	fifty-eight-year-old
sun-tanned	warm-hearted

Teacher

"Snape finished calling the names and looked up at the class. His eyes were black like Hagrid's, but they had none of Hagrid's warmth. They were cold and empty and made you think of dark tunnels.

"'You are here to learn the subtle science and exact art of potion-making,' he began. He spoke in barely more than a whisper, but they caught every word...Snape had the gift of keeping a class silent without effort."

from *Harry Potter and the Sorcerer's Stone* by J. K. Rowling

"Square-faced and square-bodied, Mr. Tanaka was my favorite teacher during three years of elementary school. His black hair had a little gray in it; he looked like a hedgehog. He always hid under his glasses and thick eyebrows. His eyes were brown, sharp, kind, and mild. His mouth had many expressions; when he was laughing, it became big and warm, but getting angry, it became tight and looked like a shellfish."

Keiko, Japan (former ESL student)

How do you picture these two teachers? Would you want Snape as your professor? Why, or why not? What about Mr. Tanaka? How do your reactions to these teachers differ?

Your assignment is to write about a teacher.

♦ Visualize your teacher. Think about: appearance, dress, voice, walk, unusual mannerisms.

♦ **Name** your teacher.

♦ Carefully choose your adjectives and verbs. Use a hyphenated modifier.

Unit 7 ♦ Best Friend
teacher's page

Objective: After thinking about the significance of a best friend in a person's life, students will write about their best friend – remembering to use vivid description.

Steps:

1. Ask the students to consider what makes another person a *best friend.* Answers may include this person makes them happy, is fun to be with, shares secrets, listens well, gives good advice.

2. Can people have more than *one* best friend during a lifetime? For example, who might be a *child's* best friend? Answers might include an invisible playmate, a relative, a pet, a stuffed animal, or another child.

3. Students will choose a best friend – from any time in their lives – to write about. How would they make this person *real* in writing? Describing what the friend looked like and giving details of their activities together will make this person genuine to the reader.

4. Pair students to introduce their best friends to each other. Distribute the handout.

Best Friend
student handout

In the classic children's book by A. A. Milne, *The House at Pooh Corner*, the little bear, Winnie the Pooh, talks about one of his best friends, Rabbit:

> "Rabbit," said Pooh to himself. "I *like* talking to Rabbit. He talks about sensible things. He doesn't use long, difficult words, like Owl. He uses short, easy words, like 'What about lunch?' and 'Help yourself, Pooh.' I suppose, *really*, I ought to go and see Rabbit."

We have talked about friends in class, and you have told a classmate about your best friend. Now, it is time to write. *Describe* your friend. (What did your friend look like?) Also, give clear *details* of what you did together or where you went. You might include a special moment in your friendship.

Objective: Students will reach back into memory to find their first romantic interest.
In writing, they will describe the person, as well as the emotions they experienced.

Steps:

1. Write "crush" on the board, and ask if anyone can define it. Some may know that as a verb, *to crush* means to press something hard. (People crush grapes with their feet to make wine.) As a noun, a *crush* is a romantic feeling for someone we don't know well. For example, a college student might have a *crush* on a professor, or a teenager on a rock star.

2. Now discuss how a *crush* is different from a *first love*. Generally, we **know** a *first love*. Our first love may be a classmate, a star athlete at school, or a neighbor. Many people develop a first love at a young age.

3. Invite the students to suggest some physical responses to a *crush* or *first love*: the heart beats fast; cheeks blush; eyes get "stars" in them; concentration is difficult.

4. Give everyone a few moments to remember their crushes or first loves. Then, ask for two or three volunteers to tell about this person and the feelings involved.

5. Distribute handout, and set the students to work!

First Love
student handout

> "Then say you'll share with me one love, one lifetime
> Let me lead you from your solitude
> Say you need me with you here, beside you
> Anywhere you go, let me go too
> Christine, that's all I ask of you."

This is part of the song, *"All I Ask Of You"* in *Phantom of the Opera* by Andrew Lloyd Webber.

Your assignment is to write about your first crush or your first love. Be sure to include a physical description of the person. Also, describe your reactions to this new experience as clearly as you can.

Unit 9 ◆ Cat, Dog, Parrot?
teacher's page

Objective: Practicing descriptive or narrative writing, or a combination, students will express their feelings about a beloved pet, or a pet they would like to own.

Materials: *(Optional)* a photograph of your pet

Steps:

1. Ask the class what animals people keep in homes in their countries, and how they feel about pets. Has anyone ever had a pet? Explain that in America, many people consider a pet almost a family member. (Show your photograph and tell about your pet, if you have one.)

2. Now ask if anyone knows what *varieties* of animals people adopt in the United States. Give examples of unusual pets your friends own, or unique ones you have read about in magazines or newspapers. Encourage reactions from the class.

3. Divide the class into groups of three to discuss pets.

4. Finally, go to the student handout. Read it, and allow about 30 minutes for writing.

Cat, Dog, Parrot?
s t u d e n t   h a n d o u t

> "For many years the cat lived in the stone house by the edge of the sea.
> He chased the wind that scuttled through the garden.
> He watched the birds flitter from tree to tree.
> At dusk he curled up in the bend of the old woman's arm.
> The old woman would scratch the cat's ears and stroke his back.
> 'Good kitty.'"
>
> from *The Cat Who Walked Across France* by Kate Banks

Have you ever owned a cat who "chased the wind" or "curled up in the bend" of your arm? Or did you ever adopt a dog, parrot, hamster, rat, rabbit, or horse? Write about a pet special to you. This could be:

- a pet you have now, or had in the past
- a friend's or a neighbor's pet
- a pet you would like to have.

Be sure to *describe* your pet. (However, if you do not like animals, you may write about those feelings!)

Unit 10 ◆ Happiness
t e a c h e r ' s   p a g e

Objective: Students will reflect on their own happiness, and write about something that has made them happy.

Steps:

1. Write the word "happy" on the board. Talk about how there are degrees of happiness and list some words in English that reflect these varying degrees (such as glad, pleased, ecstatic).

2. Distribute the handout. Tell students to write down ten things that make or have made them happy in their lives.

3. Pair students, and allow them approximately 15 minutes to discuss their lists together.

4. Have students tell the class about something that was on **their partner's** list.

5. Students will write an essay following the instructions at the bottom of the handout.

Happiness

Things that make or have made me happy in my life

1. _____
2. _____
3. _____
4. _____
5. _____
6. _____
7. _____
8. _____
9. _____
10. _____

You have listed some things that make or have made you feel happy. Choose one of these, and write about it. If it is a thing, such as a candy bar, describe the candy bar, what it is made of, and when you like to eat it. If you choose an event, describe what happened, where you were, and when it was. Include lots of details in your writing.

Unit 11 ♦ Influences: People in Our Lives
teacher's page

Objective: Students will recall significant people in their lives and will write a descriptive essay on one of them.

Steps:

1. Write the word "influence" on the board. Ask the students to define it.

2. Tell students that there are many people who influence us throughout our lives, and that these people come from many different areas, not only within our own families.

3. Divide the students into pairs. Write the following categories on the board, one at a time:

    a. Family
    b. School
    c. Work
    d. Friends

    As you write each category on the board, allow student pairs five minutes to discuss someone who has influenced them in each realm.

4. Distribute the handout, and instruct the students to write.

Influences: People in Our Lives
student handout

Write about someone who has influenced you, and explain in what way this person has done so.

Unit 12 ♦ Memories in Small Bags
t e a c h e r ' s   p a g e

Objective: Students will learn about **speed-writing** as a useful pre-writing technique.

Materials: Small bags, one for each student, or one for every two students (for a large group), and a bell

Steps:

1. Before class, fill each bag with a strip of paper, on which you have written a topic.* Place a bag on each desk. Arrange desks in a circle, if possible.

2. Write "speed-writing" on the board, and see if anyone can guess its meaning. Explain that this is a technique writers use sometimes to gather ideas. Quickly – almost without stopping – they write about a topic. Later, they refine their notes.

3. Ask the students to reach into their bags for a topic. They will write until you ring your bell. (Time allotted should be 3-5 minutes per topic.) They will then slip the strip back into the bag and pass it to the student on their right. Repeat the process until all bags have circulated. Last, students will follow the directions on the handout.

---

* Suggested topics:
- ♦ Write about your favorite neighbor as a child.
- ♦ Write about your favorite relative as a child.
- ♦ Write about your secret place as a child.
- ♦ Write about a family tradition that is important to you.
- ♦ Write about your bedroom as a child. What was unique about it?
- ♦ Write about your favorite movie as a child.
- ♦ Write about your best friend when you were ten years old.
- ♦ Write about one of the happiest moments of your life.
- ♦ Write about your favorite childhood toy or book.
- ♦ Write about your best birthday ever.
- ♦ Write about your favorite piece of clothing as a child.
- ♦ Write about your best (or worst) family vacation.

---

* This lesson was adapted from a plan by Dr. Marlene Birkman, Webster University, St. Louis, Missouri.

Memories in Small Bags
student handout

In this lesson, you learned about **speed-writing** as a pre-writing strategy. You and your classmates passed around small bags, and you wrote (quickly) about the topic in each bag. Now, from the notes you have written, choose your favorite subject. Your assignment is to expand this topic into a composition.

Unit 13 ♦ Reflections on Water
teacher's page

Objective: After reflecting on a past experience connected with water, students will write a narrative essay.

Steps:

1.   Ask students to name some bodies of water in their countries and tell how people in their countries make use of them.

2.   Mention that one of the properties of water is that it reflects images. Tell them that the word *reflect* has another meaning: to think carefully. Students should "reflect" on some water-related experience they have had and share it with a partner.

3.   Distribute the handout, and tell students to do the writing assignment.

Reflections on Water
student handout

Think about some time in your life that was related to water:

♦ Were you ever lost in a desert, thirsty, searching for a source of water?
♦ Did you ever find yourself shipwrecked on a lonely beach?
♦ Did you ever float down a big river on a raft, like Huckleberry Finn and his friend, the escaped slave, Jim?

Your water memory may not have been as adventurous as those listed above, but at some point in your life, you probably had some water-related experience. You reflected on it, and you told your partner about it. Now, write about it.

Unit 14 ♦ The Character Sketch
teacher's page

Objective: Students will see writing as an art form by comparing an artist's portrait to a writer's character sketch. They will then "paint" a person in words.

Materials: Print of a famous portrait, such as Leonardo DaVinci's *Mona Lisa*

Steps:

1. Showing the *Mona Lisa*, ask students what DaVinci needed to paint this portrait? (Paints, brushes, an easel, canvas.) Could a writer "paint" a portrait? How? What would the writer need? (Well-chosen words, pencil, a desk, paper.) Is writing, then, an art?

2. Ask for a volunteer to sit at the front of the room. Instruct the class to portray this person in words (in writing). To do this, they will describe the person, including what the person is wearing. Allow 10-15 minutes. Have several students share their writing.

3. Tell the students they have just written a *character sketch*. A character sketch introduces a person to a reader. The writer creates a "picture" of the person – telling what the person looks like, and often how this person dresses, speaks, and acts.

4. Distribute the handout; read and discuss. Then, put the students to work to complete the assignment.

The Character Sketch
student handout

A portrait, whether in painting (like the *Mona Lisa*) or in photography (as in the photo at the left), is art. In this lesson, by comparing the portrait to the character sketch, you have found that writing too is art.

Read the character studies below of two men by the American author, John Steinbeck.

> Both were dressed in denim trousers and in denim coats with brass buttons. Both wore black, shapeless hats and both carried tight blanket rolls slung over their shoulders. The first man was small and quick, dark of face, with restless eyes and sharp, strong features. Every part of him was defined; small, strong hands, slender arms, a thin and bony nose. Behind him walked his opposite, a huge man, shapeless of face, with large, pale eyes and wide, sloping shoulders; and he walked heavily, dragging his feet a little, the way a bear drags his paws.
>
> from *Of Mice and Men* by John Steinbeck

How does Steinbeck make it possible for you to *see* these men in your mind's eye? What details does he include?

_____

Your assignment now is to write a character sketch. Choose a person familiar to you, and paint this person in your words. Here are some points to consider:

- ♦ <u>Name</u> the person. This will spark interest!
- ♦ Choose your words carefully. Use details.
- ♦ Tell what this person looks like. Also tell how the person dresses, speaks, and acts.

Unit 15 ♦ Favorite Place
t e a c h e r ' s   p a g e

Objective: Students will select their favorite place and sketch a word-picture of it in writing, being particular in their choice of adjectives.

Materials: Picture postcards

Steps:

1. Give each student a picture postcard. Pair the students to describe their cards, and encourage them to come up with good adjectives. After 10-15 minutes, invite several to share their cards and descriptions. Write well-chosen adjectives on the board.

2. Tell students that their assignment will be to write about their favorite spot. (Options might include a room, a house, a beach, a wood, a secret hiding place, a small cafe.) Give the class several minutes to think quietly. Working with their partners again, they will talk about their places.

3. Distribute the handout, and discuss Arthur Golden's quote. Give the students 30 minutes to write.

Favorite Place
s t u d e n t   h a n d o u t

In our little fishing village of Yoroido, I lived in what I called a 'tipsy house.' It stood near a cliff where the wind off the ocean was always blowing. As a child it seemed to me as if the ocean had caught a terrible cold because it was always sneezing, and there would be spells when it let out a huge sneeze—which is to say there was a burst of wind with a tremendous spray. I decided our tiny house must have been offended by the ocean sneezing in its face from time to time, and it took to leaning back because it wanted to get out of the way.

from *Memoirs of a Geisha* by Arthur Golden

As you read this passage, circle the adjectives, and notice how they provide a picture of the little house. Notice also that the ocean *sneezed* and *caught a terrible cold*. Do you like Arthur Golden's description? Why, or why not?

Now, you will write about your favorite place. Describe it so exactly that your readers will feel they are standing in the spot with you. Think about your adjectives!

Unit 16 ◆ Take Your Reader Shopping
teacher's page

Objective: Students will examine "mood" as a focus in writing and incorporate this element into a piece about a favorite store.

Steps:

1. Write "mood" on the board, and see if the students can define it. (Mood is *feeling*.) A person can be in a "bad mood," or a "good mood." What about a *place*? Can a *place* have a "mood" or *feeling*? Invite input.

2. Ask the class to describe the *mood* in the classroom. Is it quiet and peaceful? Happy and excited? Worried (about the writing assignment)? How would the *mood* here differ from that of a candy store filled with children – or maybe an art museum?

3. In writing, *mood* is *feeling passed from writer to reader by description*. For this activity, the students will create mood as they write about their favorite store (as a child or as an adult) so clearly that their reader will *feel* what it was like. Give students a few minutes to gather their thoughts. Then, ask one or two to tell about "their" store.

4. Distribute the student handout. After reading it, pair the students to talk to each other about their stores. Allow 30 minutes for individual writing.

Take Your Reader Shopping
student handout

Here is a description of a store in Sandra Cisneros's book, *The House on Mango Street*.

There is a junk store. An old man owns it. The store is small with just a dirty window for light. He doesn't turn the lights on unless you got money to buy things with so in the dark we look and see all kinds of things… Tables with their feet upside-down and rows and rows of refrigerators with round corners and couches that spin dust in the air when you punch them and a hundred T.V.'s that don't work probably. Everything is on top of everything.

Notice how Cisneros creates a "mood" with her details. Does the passage make you want to visit "her" store? Below is another store, where "everything is on top of everything." See how many objects you can find. Would you like to shop here? Do you see a difference in the "mood" of the two stores?

Working to create mood, write about a store you remember. Before you begin, tell a classmate about your choice:

- ◆ What did the store look like, smell like, *feel* like?
- ◆ Did you notice any sounds when you stepped inside?
- ◆ Did you talk with people there, or did you just look around?
- ◆ Did you go alone or with someone?

Unit 17 ◆ The Gift
t e a c h e r ' s   p a g e

Objective: After considering gift-giving, students will explore a unique gift in a piece of narrative writing that includes clear description.

Materials: *(Optional)* a small gift special to the teacher

Steps:

1. First, ask the class to name occasions when people give gifts. What are some typical gifts people give each other?

2. If you have brought a special gift to class, show it and explain its importance.

3. Expand the concept of gift-giving by discussing the following as a class:

    ◆ Does a gift need to be expensive to be special?
    ◆ Can you think of "gifts" that cost no money at all? (Answers you might elicit are a bunch of field flowers, a talk that helps to solve a problem, an ocean-smoothed pebble, a child's work of art, a seashell.)
    ◆ What is the best gift you have ever received, and what made it significant?

4. Distribute the handout, and follow the instructions.

The Gift
student handout

"My bracelet's gone!" Emi screamed. "I've lost my bracelet!"…
"You know, Emi," [Mama] said. "You don't need a bracelet to remember Laurie any more than we need a photo to remember Papa or our home or all the friends and things we loved and left behind. Those are things we carry in our hearts and take with us no matter where we are sent."

from *the bracelet* by Yoshiko Uchida

Think about the passage above. Emi, a second grader, is moving from her home, and she has lost a bracelet from her best friend, Laurie. Have you ever lost a gift? Do you agree with Emi's mother, that the memory is just as important as the gift itself?

_____

In this lesson, we have talked about gifts, some expensive and others that cost no money at all, but are still "priceless."

Now, it is time for you to write about a gift. Describing it clearly will add meaning and enjoyment for your reader.

Unit 18 ♦ Mementos
teacher's page

Objective: Students will select a valued object from their past as the focal point of a personal essay.

Materials: A memento brought by the teacher

Steps:

1. Write *memento* on the board, and ask the students if they know the meaning of the word. If they do not, define it.

2. Show the students your memento, and tell them its origin and its meaning to you.

3. Ask the students to give examples of objects that people might value and save (a coin, a postcard, the pressed petals of a flower, a letter, a news clipping, a theater ticket…) Jot these on the board. Tell students to think about a memento special to them.

4. Distribute the handout, and go over it together.

5. Divide the class into groups of three to discuss their personal mementos. Allow 15 minutes for the discussion.

6. Tell the class to follow the instructions on the handout.

Mementos
student handout

Alicia and Daniel were married a year ago.

On their first anniversary, they will take the top layer of their wedding cake out of the freezer, defrost it, and share it by candlelight.

The example above illustrates how people save small objects as a reminder of the past. These objects are called **mementos.**

Think about a memento from your past. Perhaps you always keep it with you. Or maybe it's in a drawer back home. Remember, a memento is usually small and inexpensive, but its value to you is priceless.

Tell your group about the memento you have chosen to write about. Later, as you write, include these points: what the occasion was that brought the memento to you, who gave it to you, your feelings at the time, and the importance of the memento to you today.

Unit 19 ◆ Your City or Town: A Detail in Focus

teacher's page

Objective: Students will narrow their focus in writing.

Steps:

1. Name a place in your city or town special to *you*. This place can be a tourist attraction, or it might be a small and intimate coffee shop. Describe this spot clearly to your students, and explain why you love it.

2. Now, have students name their favorite places in town. List these on the board.

3. Group the students into threes. Instruct them to discuss some of the places listed. After 15-20 minutes, ask the groups which locations they considered. Did they talk about *all* of them, or did they "zero in" on one or two?

4. Point out that there are too many places to cover in one essay. Good writers stay away from topics that are too "broad." For this assignment, students should *narrow their focus* by choosing **one** of the sites listed, and write about it.

5. Distribute the handout. The class will follow the directions.

Your City or Town: A Detail in Focus
student handout

You have learned the importance of *narrowing focus* in writing. You have also talked about the numerous attractions in this city or town. Now, write about **one** of the places. Describe the location, and show with your words why you find this place so special.

Unit 20 ♦ Something for Home

teacher's page

Objective: Students will consider rich description as they write about a loved object they packed in their suitcases before a significant move to a different location.

Steps:

1. It is common these days for families to move from one place to another. Most of us have had at least one such move – to another house or apartment, a different city, a new country. Invite students to tell how many times they have moved, and how they felt.

2. Ask students to think back to the days before leaving their home. As they packed their bags, what object was so important that they could not leave it behind? A photograph? A gift? A piece of jewelry or a piece of clothing? A letter? Give the class a few moments to reminisce.

3. Request that some students describe their object to the class. Then pair the students to exchange ideas.

4. Distribute the handout. Students will follow the directions at the bottom.

Last year, when I was alone, I felt very sad. I felt lonesome, and I missed my parents a lot. Every day, especially on weekends, I was almost crying. One day when I was cleaning my closet, I found a blue sweater that was my mom's. It had a special smell that made me remember her. That sweater was impregnated with the perfume that my mother used to wear, and that odor made me feel better. Now I keep that sweater, and every time that I am homesick, I take that sweater with a special odor, and I hug it close to my heart.

Alejandra, **Mexico**
(former ESL student)

What special something did you take with you when you moved from one location to another? Was it a piece of clothing, like Alejandra's mother's sweater? A photograph? A wristwatch from your grandfather? A coin? A letter? A memorable gift? As you write about your keepsake, describe it vividly. Then, tell why it was so important that you had to have it in your suitcase.

Objective: Students will practice using transition words in an essay of comparison and contrast.

Steps:

1. Pair students. Tell them to go back in memory ten years to describe their lives then. If students are very young, they can describe their lives of three to five years ago.

2. After 15 to 20 minutes, ask students to tell the class some things their partner shared with them about their lives.

3. Write a list of transition words on the board. Tell students to use some of the transitions to compare and contrast the information they shared.

4. After students practice using transitions, distribute the handout. Tell students to follow the instructions on the handout. Remind them to use transition words in their writing.

Transition Words

Addition: also, too, in addition, moreover, besides, furthermore

Example: for example, for instance, another example is…

Differences: on the other hand, on the contrary, yet, still, but, however, in contrast, whereas, while, instead, different from, despite, in spite of, even though

Similarities: in the same way, both/and, neither/nor, not only/ but also, similar to, alike, likewise

Consequence: as a result, consequently, so then, therefore, thus

Conclusion: in conclusion, in summary, to summarize, finally

Changes

I was as normal as the other children in my neighborhood. Like my friends, I used to go to school and play soccer and basketball. Not only did we play at school, but when we came back home, we also played soccer, yo-yo, and "trompo" in the street.

My life ten years ago and my life now are alike because I live with my parents and brother and sister, and also, I'm going to school. However, now I'm worried about money, the future, and getting older. This is different from my childhood, when I was worried about nothing except some test.

I've had many external changes, such as getting taller and thinner, even though many people think I looked the same as I do today. On the other hand, some interesting internal changes have occurred. Some can be easily detected, and some others people will never figure out.

Changes are good in life, even though they sometimes don't look good at first sight. But after some time, they start making sense in my life. Instead of being afraid of changes, I have to make them serve my purpose.

*Byron, **Guatemala***

You know that the way your life is today is different from the past. And you know that in the future, your life will change in some ways. Do you welcome change, as Byron does?

With your partner, you shared memories of your life in the past. Think about how different you are today from that time. Also, think about what you have learned and what you have done since that time.

Write a composition comparing and contrasting your life of today and your life of five or ten years ago.

Unit 22 ◆ Strange Encounters of a New Kind
teacher's page

Objective: Students will produce a four-paragraph essay after practicing brainstorming and reviewing the structure of an essay.

Steps:

1. Ask the students to think about a move they had to make in their lives. Then ask them to recall the changes they had to make in their lives after such a move, whether the move was to another country, a city in the same country, or a move within the same city. Give students time to recall the differences between their previous location and the new one and how they felt about them. Were these differences exciting, or did they seem strange and uncomfortable?

2. Invite several students to share some of the differences they thought of and to express their feelings about them. Next, pair students to brainstorm (on paper) three things they *liked* about the new location and three things they *disliked* about the new location.

3. Distribute the handout. Point out the essay structure outlined at the bottom on the page, and direct students to write a four-paragraph essay.

Strange Encounters of a New Kind
student handout

> "Delightful" was Gopal's new word. "London is delightful,"
> he wrote home. "The college is delightful, Professor
> William Morgan is delightful and so is Mrs. Morgan and the
> little Morgans...The hostel is delightful...I find my work delightful."
>
> from *The Oyster* by Rumer Godden

The above quote is about a young man from Bengal who left home to study in England. Were you excited, as Gopal was, when you moved? Or were you unhappy because everything was different and unfamiliar?

Using the four-paragraph format, write a composition expressing your feelings:

Introduction

(Body) What I Liked and Why

(Body) What I Didn't Like and Why

Conclusion

Unit 23 ◆ Conversation – A Lost Art?
teacher's page

Objective: After deciding if conversation is a "lost art" these days, students will appraise its value in writing.

Steps:

1. Ask the students to define *conversation.* Then ask if they think that conversation is an "art" that needs to be taught and practiced before someone becomes "good" at it? *Or* do people naturally know how to converse? Invite discussion.

2. Many people today in America feel that meaningful conversations have been replaced by TV, video games, social networking (Facebook, MySpace, Twitter), texting, Skyping, Instant Messaging, etc. Dinnertime, once an important meal when families talked, has been replaced by eating in shifts or by fast food grabbed before hurrying to activities.

   Put students into groups of three to exchange ideas on the importance placed on conversation in their countries and/or in their homes.

3. Distribute the handout, and go from there!

Conversation – A Lost Art?
student handout

> She liked to call on him at the garage and talk to him in his greasy office with its piles of receipts and orders for spare parts. She liked to drink tea from one of his mugs with the greasy fingerprints on the outside…Mr. J. L. B. Matekoni enjoyed these sessions. They would talk about Mochudi, or politics, or just exchange the news of the day. He would tell her who was having trouble with his car, and what was wrong with it, and who had bought petrol that day, and where they said they were going.
>
> from *The No. 1 Ladies Detective Agency* by Alexander McCall Smith

It's easy to visualize the gentle, slow-paced conversation between two friends in a car repair shop above. We talked in this class about whether or not conversation is an art. Perhaps it is quickly becoming a "lost" art? What is your opinion?

Now, you will write your views on *conversation*. Here are the suggested topics:

- ♦ Conversation, a Lost Art?
  or
- ♦ Conversation in My Family
  or
- ♦ A Conversation Special to Me

Unit 24 ♦ Rain
teacher's page

Objective: Students will learn about creating pictures in words and will then practice *imagery* as they write about rain.

Steps:

1. Ask students what emotions they experience on a rainy day. Do they feel peaceful… relaxed…depressed…lazy…frightened sometimes?

2. What might they see or hear on a rainy day? Encourage discussion. Then, explain that when writers create powerful or beautiful "pictures" for their readers, this is called *imagery*. Ask the class to listen for "images" as you read the following, written by a college ESL student.

> *It's a rainy day. I decide to stay home. It's boring for me. When I look out my window, I see an interesting picture below. Everyone has an umbrella—black, red, yellow—like many roofs walking on the street! Some children run in the rain and play games. Someone forgot an umbrella and is dripping wet. He looks helpless. I have found a good thing to do on a rainy day. I can observe people. I don't feel bored anymore.*

   What did the class "see" in the writing? (Answers you hope to elicit are a soft rain, playing children, a lonely man, colorful umbrellas – like roofs walking!)

3. Distribute the handout. Read and discuss together. Students will write a rainy-day memory that includes imagery.

Rain

Days of sunshine had melted the snow in the field, and a brief rain had rinsed everything clean...Shortly, the kitchen door opened and his mother's hands came to rest on his shoulders. They listened to the water drip from the trees.

"I like that sound," she said, "I used to sit here and listen to water run off the roof like that before you were born."

from *The Story of Edgar Sawtelle*
by David Wroblewski

The day continued as stormy as it had begun. The rain fell in sheets and the wind whipped it...The rain barrels outside were overflowing and the rain from the roof gurgled into their fullness...the deluge came again, as violent as before.

from *The Yearling*
by Marjorie Kinnan Rawlings

In the two passages above, the authors create very different pictures (or images) of rain. What do you *see* when you read the first? The second? What do you *hear* in each? How are the *feelings* very different?

Your assignment is to bring back a rainy-day memory and to include clear images with your words.

Unit 25 ♦ Snow
teacher's page

Objective: Students will recognize similes and metaphors and will use at least one of them in their writing about *snow*.

Steps:

1. This lesson works especially well during – or following – the first winter snow. Ask your students if snow falls in their countries, and invite them to share their feelings about snow.

2. Next, write *simile* and *metaphor* on the board, and explain. A *simile* compares two different things using the word *like* or *as*. For example, "I felt *like a child* when I first saw snow" is a *simile*. A *metaphor* describes something by calling it something else. "Snow was *a soft white blanket* covering the fields" is a *metaphor*. Writers use similes and metaphors to paint word-pictures.

3. Expand on similes and metaphors by asking students to guess what is meant when someone "works like a horse" or "eats like a pig," or when someone is called a rat, a little mouse, a snake, or a fox.

4. Distribute the handout. Students will follow the instructions on the handout.

As lesson reinforcement, the teacher might copy the students' similes and metaphors and post them in the room for the next class.

Snow
student handout

There was no wind. The trees stood still as giant statues. And the moon was so bright the sky seemed to shine. Somewhere behind us a train whistle blew, long and low, like a sad, sad song.

from *Owl Moon* by Jane Yolen

Outside the wind blew steadily from the north, driving snow against the courthouse. By noon, three inches had settled on the town.... It swirled up and down Amity Harbor streets.

from *Snow Falling on Cedars* by David Guterson

Can you find four similes in the passages above? You have learned that similes and metaphors provide readers with word-pictures.

Now see if you can include at least one simile or metaphor in your writing about

♦ Snow

♦ Snow in My Country

♦ A Snow Memory

Unit 26 ♦ Choose Your Season
teacher's page

Objective: After exploring similes and metaphors, students will include one or more in an essay on their favorite season of the year.

Steps:

1. For this lesson, students will write about their favorite season. Ask two or three students to tell you their favorite and to explain why they love it.

2. Now write *simile* and *metaphor* on the board. Remind students that these are words used in unique ways that add variety to description. (A *simile* compares two things, using *like* or *as*; a *metaphor* compares two things without using *like* or *as*.) Give examples of each.

3. Teach the class that it is <u>very</u> important to use fresh and original similes and metaphors. (Warn the class about clichés, if you feel that is appropriate.) Ask a student who loves winter to come up with a creative *cold as...* or *clear as....* Ask another to describe summer as *hot as...*

4. Go to the handout, and set the students to complete it. Ask them to share answers with a partner before writing.

Choose Your Season
s t u d e n t   h a n d o u t

Your assignment is to write about your favorite season and to include at least one simile or metaphor. See how imaginative you can be as you complete these metaphors:

♦ Spring is …
    ♦ Summer is …
        ♦ Fall is …
            ♦ Winter is …

Now, try creating similes. Use your favorite season.

♦ Summer looks like…
♦ Summer tastes like…
♦ Summer feels like…
♦ Summer smells like…
♦ Summer sounds like…

Discuss your favorite season with a partner before you begin writing about it.

II. Writing with the Five Senses

Unit 1 ♦ Are You Listening?
teacher's page

Objective: After reviewing the importance of using the five senses in writing, students will zero in on the sense of *hearing*.

Steps:

1. Review the five senses. Write them on the board. To make writing more interesting, writers often tell what something *looks* like, *feels* like, *tastes* like, *smells* like, and/or *sounds* like. In this lesson, students will focus on *sounds*.

2. Choosing at least two of the following, ask the students to imagine themselves:

   ♦ Walking along a busy city street. *What do they hear?*
   ♦ Walking along a dark deserted country road late at night. *What do they hear?*
   ♦ Walking silently through the woods on a sunny morning. *What do they hear?*
   ♦ Sitting with a large family around the dinner table. *What do they hear?*

3. Distribute the handout; read it together. Next, pair the students; give them 15 minutes to tell each other a memory based on some *sound(s)*.

4. Following the handout directions, students will write for 30 minutes. When finished, the same partners (as in #3) will read their essays to each other. They should *listen* carefully, and offer feedback, comments, and/or suggestions.

Are You Listening?
student handout

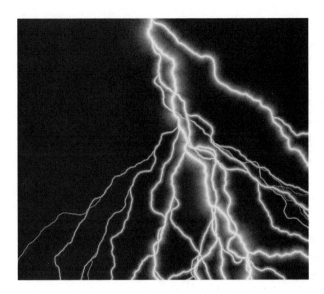

> On sultry summer days at my grandma's farm in Michigan, the air gets damp and heavy. Stormclouds drift low over the fields. Birds fly close to the ground. The clouds glow for an instant with a sharp, crackling light, and then a roaring, low, tumbling sound of thunder makes the windows shudder in their panes. The sound used to scare me when I was little... I feared the sound of thunder more than anything. I always hid under the bed when the storm moved near the farmhouse.
>
> from *Thunder Cake* by Patricia Polacco

Can you recall a sound that frightened you as a child (or as an adult), as thunder frightened this author? On the other hand, perhaps some sound was (or is) comforting to you. Share your experience with a classmate, and then listen carefully to your classmate's story. When you finish, begin writing your essay, paying attention to the *sound(s)* you remember.

Unit 2 ◆ Smell and Memory
teacher's page

Objective: After thinking about the smells that surround them every day, students will write about a smell that connects them to a distinct memory.

Steps:

1. Remind the students that in the unit, **Are You Listening?**, you talked about how writers use the five senses. Reviewing each one briefly, ask students for examples of how this sense gives us pleasure. (Sometimes, of course, the senses can convey disgust, alarm, or fear, such as the smell of spoiled potatoes, the taste of an unfamiliar food, the sound of a tornado.)

2. This lesson will center on *smell*. Students will take paper and, *in five minutes*, will write all the smells they remember – good or bad – since they got up this morning. Allow for sharing time. (Students will probably amaze themselves at the length of their lists!)

3. Next, the students will go back farther (than the morning) in their lives to recall an unforgettable smell, pleasant or unpleasant. Give them time to do this quietly.

4. Distribute the handout. Discuss it. Then, for about 15 minutes, pair the students to share the memory they have chosen.

Smell and Memory
student handout

Below is a passage from the book, ***Rascal***. Notice how the author, Sterling North, uses *smell* in his description.

> Returning to school has always been a pleasure. It meant new pencils and composition books—the pencils smelling of cedar as you sharpened them. Most of the texts were dog-eared and scrawled with unfunny comments and crude drawings. But occasionally we were furnished two or three books fresh from the presses, fragrant of new paper and printers' ink.

Experts say that *smell* is the sense most closely connected with memory. You have just *sharpened* this sense by writing the smells you recall since getting up this morning. You have also reached back into your past to recall a meaningful smell. Your assignment now is to write about your memory.

Unit 3 ♦ Touch!
t e a c h e r ' s   p a g e

Objective: As they consider the importance of the sense of touch, students will examine in writing a memory focusing on touch.

Materials: A carry-bag filled with interesting-to-the-touch objects: a leaf, a smooth pebble, tree bark, swatches of fabric (velvet, satin, and silk), sandpaper, a cotton ball, a washcloth

Steps:

1. Pair the students. Give each pair an object from your carry-bag. Allow them time to gather adjectives that describe how their object *feels*. Then, go around the class, collecting descriptors and writing them on the board.

2. Remind the students how important it is for them, as writers, to exercise their senses. In this class, they have been thinking about *touch*. Now see if anyone can recall a memory concerning touch. Ask two or three to share.

3. Read the handout. Assign the students to again work with their partners to tell their "touch" stories before writing.

Touch!
s t u d e n t   h a n d o u t

> Use your eyes as if tomorrow you would become blind. Hear the music of voices, the song of a bird, as if you would become deaf tomorrow. Touch each object as if tomorrow you would never be able to feel anything again. Smell the perfume of the flowers and taste with true enjoyment each bite of food as if tomorrow you would never be able to smell and taste again.
>
> *Helen Keller, author, blind and deaf from two years of age*

As children, we heard the words, "Don't touch!" when we got too close to a hot stove, or visited a gift shop with a grown-up. Now as adults however, think of the pleasure we get when we touch a child's face, hug a friend, or feel a piece of clothing!

As writers, we cannot remind ourselves too often to *use the five senses*. In this lesson, our focus has been *touch*. Your assignment is to relate a time when *touch* was significant in your life.

Unit 4 ♦ Spring's Here!
teacher's page

Objective: As students take a walk outside together, they will put their senses to work as they skillfully observe their surroundings. Later, they will report their findings in writing.

Steps:

1.   Choose a beautiful spring day. Invite students to tell some interesting ways that people in their countries celebrate spring's appearing. Tell the class that Americans pack away winter clothes, take on "spring cleaning," plant vegetables, hunt for mushrooms, picnic, attend outside concerts, and often venture outside to take a walk.

2.   Direct the students to think about this last activity. How might using their five senses make a walk more enjoyable? For example, if they *looked* carefully, what might they *see*? If they *listened* intently, what might they *hear?* If they paid attention to aromas, what might they *smell?* In a few moments, the class will practice using their senses while taking a walk together outside with their teacher.

3.   Distribute the student handout. Read it, and pay special attention to the **RULES** for this event.

Spring's Here!

> "The way to go wildflowering is not to gather them, but to love them, to leave them, and to bring their beauty home in one's heart.
>
> "The most beautiful thing we can witness is the mysterious. It is the source of all true art and science. He to whom this emotion is a stranger, who can no longer pause to wonder and stand in awe, is as good as dead; his eyes are closed."
>
> *Albert Einstein*

Let's go outside with our eyes wide open, ready to "pause" and "wonder." Take a pencil and paper with you. We will walk around school for about thirty minutes.

RULES:

❖ Don't say a word to anyone. Silence!
❖ Utilize your senses. *Look. Listen. Smell. Touch.* Maybe even *taste*!
❖ Absorb your surroundings, as a sponge soaks up spilled water.
❖ Take notes as you walk. Write whatever your senses are telling you.

When you return to class, you will use the notes you gathered on your walk to complete the writing assignment. Title your paper *A Walk Outside School.*

Unit 5 ◆ Chocolate Chip Cookie Day
teacher's page

Objective: Students will focus on a simple subject and then use some or all of the five senses to enrich their writing.

Materials: Chocolate chip cookies

Steps:

1. On the board write:
    ☞ Keep your subject specific and simple.
    ☞ Use one or more of the five senses in writing.

2. Ask students to think of one simple thing or activity that makes them happy. The thing must not cost more than a meal at McDonald's. Ask each student to share with the class. Explain that a whole composition could be written about a simple topic like any of the activities or things they mentioned. Referring to the second item you wrote on the board, tell students how good writers often use one or more of the five senses so that their readers can join into the experience as they read.

3. Distribute the handout. Read and discuss Part 1.

4. Give a chocolate chip cookie to each student.

5. Divide the class into pairs or groups of three. Tell them to follow the instructions in Part 2. Allow students 10 or 15 minutes for discussion, and then have them share their ideas with the class.

6. Direct the students to write an essay about one of the topics below:

    ◆ Cookies
    ◆ A Cookie Memory
    ◆ A Cookie in My Country

Chocolate Chip Cookie Day
student handout

1

Descriptive writing, in which a writer describes an object, place, person, etc., is one of the best and most enjoyable types of writing. One of the ways to make descriptive writing richer is to use some or all of the five senses. A writer can tell how something *looks*, *feels*, *tastes*, *smells*, or *sounds* so clearly that the reader can almost see, feel, taste, smell, or hear the things described.

2

You are going to practice *using some of the five senses* in your writing while you *keep your topic simple*. Below are some questions to guide your discussion:

- ♦ How does the cookie look?
- ♦ How does the cookie feel?
- ♦ How does the cookie smell?
- ♦ Does the cookie have a sound?
- ♦ How does the cookie taste? (You can take a bite!)
- ♦ What is the cookie used for?
- ♦ On what occasion is a chocolate chip cookie special?

III. Writing Around the Holidays

Unit 1 ♦ Writing from the Heart
teacher's page

Objective: Students will recognize that good writing often comes *from the heart.* They will write (from their heart) about a Valentine.

Materials: Cutout paper hearts, two of each color, and chocolate hearts

Steps:

1. Ask students whether Valentine's Day – or any type of holiday associated with romance – is celebrated in their countries, and if so, how? Invite discussion. (The Appendix contains a history of Valentine's Day, which may be copied and distributed.)

2. Explain that writers often write best when focusing on something (or someone) very familiar to them; this is writing "from the heart."

3. Give out the paper hearts, one to each student. Students will find partners by matching their colors. Next, distribute the student handout, and set the class to work.

4. At the end of this activity, hand each student a chocolate heart in return for the completed composition.

Writing from the Heart

You have found the classmate whose paper heart matches yours. With this partner, talk about a "Valentine" special to you. Here are the choices:

- ♦ My Wife or My Husband
- ♦ My Girlfriend or My Boyfriend
- ♦ The Love of My Life

After 15 minutes of sharing together, it will be time to write about your choice.

Unit 2 ♦ Heroes in History
teacher's page

Objective: Students will write a biography of one of their national heroes, either real or fictional – *or* about a personal "hero" in their lives.

Steps:

1. Plan this lesson as near to Presidents' Day as possible. Ask the students if they know why Presidents' Day is celebrated in the United States and which presidents are featured. Tell a little about George Washington and Abraham Lincoln, or copy the handout in the Appendix for the class.

2. Ask students to define the word "hero." Then direct them to name some heroes, real (Mahatma Gandhi) or imaginary (Superman).

3. Group students into threes. They will name a hero from their country *or* someone who has been a "hero" to them in their lives. Instruct them to share stories about their heroes.

4. After 15-20 minutes, distribute and read the handout. Have the students begin writing.

Heroes in History

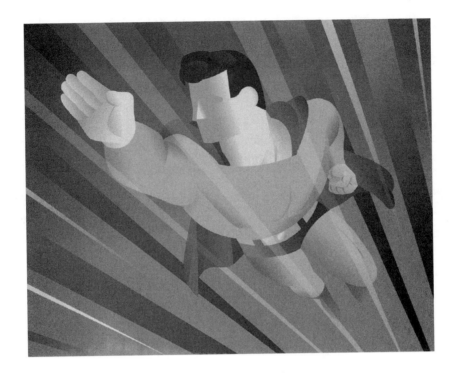

You and your classmates have talked about people who are heroes in your cultures because of what they believed in and because of their actions. Write about a hero from your country. *Or*, if you prefer, you may write about someone who is a "hero" to you.

Unit 3 ♦ St. Patrick's Day
teacher's page

Objective: Students will describe one of their national holidays.

Materials: Objects and/or pictures representative of St. Patrick's Day

Steps:

1. Explain the origins of St. Patrick's Day, and how it is celebrated in the United States. (See Appendix for explanation, which can also be used as a student handout.)

2. Divide the students into pairs. Have them tell their partner about one of their national holidays. They should describe how it is celebrated and its background. Allow students 15 minutes to share.

3. Tell students to follow the instructions on the handout.

St. Patrick's Day
student handout

Write about one of your national holidays. Describe the origin of the holiday (why is it celebrated), and what people do on this day.

Unit 4 ♦ Boo!
teacher's page

Objective: In small groups, students will create Halloween stories enlivened by the use of newly-learned "Halloween verbs."

Materials: *(Optional)* pumpkins for carving and small candles

Steps:

1. *Ask students to call out as many words connected with Halloween as they can. Write these on the board. Then add (and define) some colorful *verbs* associated with this night, such as *scream, screech, howl, shriek, wail, groan,* and *moan.*

2. Distribute the handout. Read together, pointing out the author's carefully selected verbs.

3. Divide the students into groups of three. They will follow the directions at the bottom of the handout, as they spin their Halloween tales.

4. *(Optional)* The following class, provide pumpkins for the students to carve. Then, place the lit jack-o-lanterns around the class, and turn out the lights. By flashlight, read the stories written by the students.

* You may wish to copy the Halloween handout in the Appendix at some point during this lesson.

Boo!

Owl said,
"Door, why do you slam?"
Door said,
"It is a dark and stormy night.
Ghost wails
Stool thumps
Broom swishes
Candle flickers
Fire smokes
Window rattles
Floor creaks
and so I slam."
Owl said,
"Then I shall hoot."
And Owl began to HOOT.

from *Old Devil Wind* by Bill Martin, Jr.

Do you like this passage? How do the author's words create pictures for you as you read?

Including at least three new words you learned in this class, work with your group to create a scary Halloween story. Begin, "One dark and stormy night…"

Unit 5 ♦ Ghost Stories
teacher's page

Objective: After thinking about the ghost story genre around the world – and about how ghosts appear in literature – students will either compose a ghost story or relate a scary experience in writing.

Steps:

1. Ask the students if ghost stories are popular in their countries:

    ☞ Do people believe in ghosts?
    ☞ When and where are ghost stories told?
    ☞ Are ghosts found in the literature of their countries?

2. Point out that, in English, ghosts appear in Shakespeare's *Hamlet* and *Macbeth,* in Washington Irving's *The Legend of Sleepy Hollow*, in Charles Dickens's *A Christmas Carol*, and in J. K. Rowling's *Harry Potter*.

3. Divide the class into groups of three to share ghost stories. After approximately 10-15 minutes, invite two or three students to briefly share their stories.

4. Distribute the handout. Students will follow the directions on the handout. If anyone cannot come up with a ghost story, that person can choose the third option.

Ghost Stories
student handout

Ghost stories abound in the United States. The ghost of Mary Todd Lincoln, Abraham Lincoln's widow, is believed to haunt one of the bedrooms in the White House. In St. Charles County, Missouri, people say that the ghost of Daniel Boone's wife (with her head tucked under her arm) rides horseback at night near the old Boone home.

In a popular ghost story, called *The Vanishing Hitchhiker,* a young man picks up a beautiful hitchhiker late one evening. As he drives her home, she complains of being cold, so he gives her his sweater. The next day, realizing she didn't give him his sweater back, the young man returns to her house. Her father answers the door and tells the young man, "My daughter died a year ago." The young man goes to the nearby cemetery – and finds his sweater hanging on her gravestone.

After you have told ghost stories in your group, choose one of the following topics to write about:

 ♦ An original ghost story (that you create)
 ♦ A traditional ghost story from your culture
 ♦ A scary experience

Unit 6 ♦ Voyages and Thanksgiving
teacher's page

Objective: Students will learn about and apply the comparison and contrast technique as they first think of themselves as "pilgrims" and then chronicle their "voyages" to America.

Steps:

1. Write the word "Thanksgiving" on the board, and invite the students to share what they know about this American holiday.

2. Explain the background of this holiday to the class (or use the handout in the Appendix).

3. Write the words *similarities/comparison* and *differences/contrast* on the board. Point out that there are similarities and differences between the Pilgrims' voyage and their own trips to America. Explain that comparison and contrast are used in writing to analyze two situations.

4. Pair students, and distribute the handout. Students will practice comparison and contrast as they go through the list of questions. Allow students 10 to 15 minutes to talk. Afterwards, ask each pair to share something they have learned about their partners.

5. Direct students to use comparison and contrast to write an essay about one of the topics below:

    ♦ My First Impressions of America
    ♦ My Trip to America
    ♦ The Pilgrims and I

Thanksgiving Parallel

(similarities, differences)

1. How did you come to America or this city? By airplane?
2. At what time of the year did you arrive?
3. What did you bring with you?
4. Who came with you?
5. Before you came, did you worry about anything?
6. Is this the city or town you wanted to come to? Why, or why not?
7. Is the weather what you expected?
8. Did you have a place to live when you came here?
9. Did someone help you? Who?
10. What new foods did you find in your new home? Were they very different from the foods you were used to?

IV. Writing with the Imagination

Unit 1 ♦ Finding Beauty in the Ordinary
teacher's page

Objective: After searching for something beautiful in a familiar object, students will relate their feelings about it in a descriptive or narrative paper.

Materials: A carry-bag filled with some of Saroyan's "things" (Please refer to the quote on the student handout.)

Steps:

1. Ask the students to name some things they consider beautiful – and why. These might include a pearl ring, a painting, a rose, a starry night, a colorful sunset, a piece of furniture. Tell them that in this activity, you will encourage them to expand their ideas about beauty. Could an insect be beautiful? A button? An egg?

2. From your carry-bag, take out the objects, one by one, asking the students if they can find beauty in each one. Have them explain the beauty they see.

3. Distribute the handout; read and discuss it. Students will then follow the instructions at the bottom of the handout. Allow about 30 minutes of writing time.

Finding Beauty in the Ordinary
student handout

Below is a quote from Pulitzer Prize-winning author William Saroyan. A father tells his son that every house should have an "art table." Curious, the boy asks what would be on the table.

> "A leaf. A coin. A button. A stone. A small piece of torn newspaper. An apple. An egg. A pebble. A flower. A dead insect. A shoe."
>
> "Everybody's *seen* those things."
>
> "Of course. But nobody *looks* at them, and that's what art is. To look at familiar things as if they had never before been seen. A plain sheet of paper with typing on it. A necktie. A pocketknife. A key. A fork. A cup. A bottle. A bowl. A walnut."
>
> "Leaf" from *Papa, You're Crazy*

Pick a simple, everyday object – either from the list above, or select another – and *look at it* with fresh eyes. Your teacher will pair you with another student to talk about your choices and to share ideas.

Then, please describe it in your paper, or write a story about it.

Unit 2 ♦ An Imaginary Trip to an Art Museum
teacher's page

Objective: Students will write a personal response to a work of art

Materials: Pictures of works of art: paintings, sculptures; classic, contemporary, primitive pieces

Steps:

1. Ask students if they do anything creative (painting, drawing, poetry, music). Ask them how they feel as they do their work, and how they hope people will react to their work.

2. Show the students one of the pictures of art you brought. Ask several students to describe what they see and their feelings about it.

3. After receiving several responses, tell the students they have been "brainstorming" and explain how brainstorming is used in writing.

4. Group students in threes. Distribute the student handout. Then, pass around the pictures of artwork, and allow students to discuss their responses with their group.

5. After 15 minutes of small-group work, have students share their responses with the class. Finally, they will follow the directions at the bottom of the handout.

An Imaginary Trip to an Art Museum
student handout

You will practice brainstorming as you take an imaginary trip to an art museum. Look at the pictures of works of art in museums from all over the world that your teacher will pass around, and share your ideas about the pictures with your group.

As you look at each photograph, think about the following:

☞ Do you like it?
☞ How does it make you feel?
☞ Does it bring back a memory to you?

After you complete your imaginary trip, choose one of the works of art you viewed, and write about:

◆ your impressions

or

◆ a memory the picture brings to your mind

Unit 3 ♦ Drawing into Writing
teacher's page

Objective: Students will exercise their imagination, first to create a mental image from a single line, and then to build a story around it.

Materials: A copy of either *The Missing Piece* or *The Missing Piece Meets the Big O* by Shel Silverstein

Steps:

1. Draw a simple line on the board: curved, straight, squiggly, wavy. Ask the class to imagine an object or a person from that line.

2. Let the students choose the best object or person imagined, and invite them to expand the idea by telling a story. Several students can contribute, using the "chain story" approach, until they agree they are finished.

3. Show the class either of the Silverstein books suggested above, which demontrates how a piece of writing can come from simple line drawings.

4. Distribute the handout, and instruct the students to choose a line. As the class did, they will first visualize an object or a person in that line, and then create their story.

5. Allow 30 minutes for writing. If time allows, ask some students to read their stories to the class.

Drawing into Writing
student handout

Your writing assignment is to choose one of the three lines below. Think about your choice until an object or a person comes to mind. Then, write a story based on your line.

1.

2.

3.

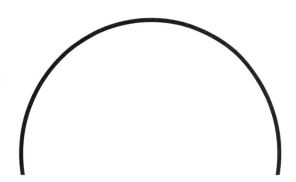

Unit 4 ♦ What Am I?
teacher's page

Objective: Without naming a familiar object, students will describe it so vividly through personification that its identity will be clear to the reader.

Materials: A carry bag filled with everyday items, such as a wallet, a woman's purse, a pencil, a pair of sunglasses, a key, a seashell, a box of matches, a bottle of perfume, a comb, an eraser

Steps:

1. Write "personification" on the board, and ask if anyone knows its meaning. Personification is writing about an object or an animal as if it were a person. For example, in Snow White and the Seven Dwarfs, the mirror answers the wicked queen. In another story, Little Red Riding Hood, the wolf speaks.

2. Remove the objects from your carry bag, one at a time, and set them on a table. Students delight in watching things emerge from bags!

3. Distribute the student handout. Students will follow the instructions on it. They will title their papers, "What Am I?" and will write one paragraph only. They will not name their choice! Allow 15-20 minutes for writing.

4. Group the students into threes. Students in each group will read their paragraphs one by one, while the other two in the group attempt to identify the object personified. Ask each group to read at least one description to the class.

What Am I?

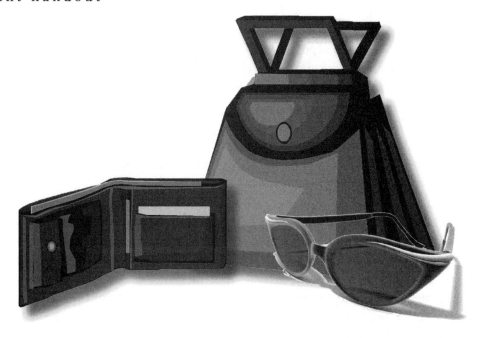

You have learned about the enjoyable type of writing called *personification*. Personification in writing tells about an object or an animal as if it were human, with human thoughts and characteristics.

Choose one object from your teacher's bag to write about. Don't point at it or show other students what you have chosen. Imagine that you *are* that object. Write describing yourself, but do not mention the name of the thing you are personifying.

Here are some descriptive elements you might include in your writing:

- ◆ Color
- ◆ Shape
- ◆ Size
- ◆ Smell (if there is one)
- ◆ Texture (rough, smooth, hard, soft)
- ◆ Uses
- ◆ Cost

Unit 5 ♦ I Am A...
teacher's page

Objective: Students will take the "point of view" of their favorite animal or insect to write a story focusing on one day in its life.

Steps:

1. Tell your class that good writers put themselves into the characters they portray, to decide how these characters move, think, and act. Sometimes they do this with animals, and when they do, this is called *personification*.

2. Read the book excerpt from the student handout, and see if your students can guess the animal.

3. Next, ask several students to name their favorite animal or insect. Choosing one, encourage the class to consider how this animal or insect moves, and what it might think about and *do* during the day (or night), what it might eat, see, smell, and hear. Repeat the process with another creature, if helpful.

4. Pair the students to talk about their favorite animals. They should help each other to gather more ideas.

5. Distribute the handout. Read it together. Students will then follow instructions on the handout.

I Am A...

...I lap from china bowls.
I clean off dishes.
I like the taste of cream,
But while I drink I dream
Of birds and fishes.
In the dark of the night,
I sing as I creep along walls.
In the bright
        morning light,
I mew as I
        saunter down halls.

from *I Walk at Night* by Lois Duncan

...A little boy is living in the house, and he likes to read about spiders (like me!)...The first time I met him, I was inside the house. He found me and took me outside. He was playing with me in his fingers and blowing me away from his hand. I like my web, and I think I can sleep now because nobody will get into my web until morning.

Svetlana, **Russia**
(former ESL student)

In class, we defined *personification*. Also, you discussed your favorite animal or insect with a classmate. Now, your task is to *write* as if you *are* that creature. (Choose one day or one night only, as Svetlana did.) Consider:

♦ As a _____ (animal or insect), what would I think and *do*?
♦ What might I eat, see, smell, and hear?

Unit 6 ♦ Folktales and Storytelling
teacher's page

Objective: Students will understand the historical movement from oral to written communication and will practice the two forms, first by telling a folktale and then by writing it.

Steps:

1. Write the word *folktale* on the board and ask the students if they know what a folktale is. Give an example by telling an American folktale, such as Johnny Appleseed, Rip Van Winkle, or Paul Bunyan. Or you could choose Cinderella or Little Red Riding Hood, as fairytales are a form of folktale. (Choose a story you love, and tell it well.)

2. Ask students to think about a folktale from their culture. Assign each student a partner, and have them exchange folktales.

3. Distribute handout.

Folktales and Storytelling
student handout

Folktales began as an oral tradition, told from one generation to the next, parents to children. They exist in every region of the world. Some of the stories are not about real people, but about magical characters, like fairies, witches, and talking animals. Others tell about actual people, but their lives are exaggerated.

The United States is a relatively young country. Its folk stories come from people who settled here years ago and brought stories with them, from Native American tribes (Indians), and from tales that developed as the country grew.

You and a classmate have told each other a folktale from your culture. Now, it is time to write that folktale, or a different folktale from your country.

Unit 7 ◆ One More Frog and Toad
teacher's page

Objective: After listening to a story about Frog and Toad, students will realize the value of simple writing. They will then create their own Frog and Toad adventure, using dialogue to make the characters more real.

Materials: A Frog and Toad book by Arnold Lobel

Steps:

1. Invite students to remember their best childhood friend. Ask them to share some fun they enjoyed together, such as: swimming in a lake, riding bikes, exploring the woods, building a snowman, catching fireflies at night, playing computer games.

2. Introduce them to two best friends in children's literature, Frog and Toad. These two find *simple* adventures in Arnold Lobel's books, written over 35 years ago, and still enjoyed today. Read one of the stories, pointing out the charm of *dialogue.**

3. To add variety to dialogue, encourage students to minimize use of "say" and "tell." Suggest synonyms, like *shout, yell, holler, answer, add, promise, explain, reply, whisper, complain.*

4. Distribute the student handout. Students will examine punctuation placement in the dialogue at the top of the page. If needed, explain rules for quoted speech.

* If you cannot find a *Frog and Toad* book, go online to Google. Key in *Frog and Toad excerpt* to find quotations and illustrations from "The Garden." From this and other sites, you can copy the text and pictures from a few pages and print them so that you can read them with your students in class. This is legal "fair use" of copyrighted material.
Or go to *Frog and Toad Are Friends excerpts* to discover 4-minute videos of "The Letter," "A Swim," "Dragons and Giants," and others, videos you can show your class.

One More Frog and Toad
student handout

> Toad was sitting on his front porch. Frog came along and said, "What is the matter, Toad? You are looking sad."
>
> "Yes," said Toad. "This is my sad time of day. It is the time when I wait for the mail to come. It always makes me very unhappy."
>
> "Why is that?" asked Frog.
>
> "Because I never get any mail," said Toad.
>
> "Not ever?" asked Frog.
>
> "No, never," said Toad. "No one has ever sent me a letter. Every day my mailbox is empty. That is why waiting for the mail is a sad time for me." Frog and Toad sat on the porch, feeling sad together.
>
> from "The Letter"
> in *Frog and Toad Are Friends* by Arnold Lobel

Your assignment is to write another story about Frog and Toad. This will be a good exercise in keeping your writing simple. Use dialogue, as speech will give a closer look into the characters.

Before you write, talk with a classmate about your best childhood friend and about some adventures you shared. One of these might be the basis for the Frog and Toad episode you tell.

Unit 8 ♦ Make a PB and J
teacher's page

Objective: Students will enjoy a taste of *expository writing*. After giving directions on how to make a pb and j sandwich, they will choose a "how to" and write the process.

Materials: A loaf of bread, a jar of peanut butter, a jar of jelly, a spreading knife, a sandwich board, and (optional) plastic gloves. Also, several pre-made pb & j sandwiches, quartered and plastic-wrapped.

Steps:

1. Invite the students to instruct you, step by step, how to assemble an American staple, a peanut butter and jelly sandwich. Spread out your supplies. Explain that you will say nothing, but that you will do *exactly* what they say. (This can be funny. If, for example, they tell you to put the p.b. on the bread, place the jar on top of the loaf!)

2. Once the task is completed, pass around the quarter sandwiches, and let everyone sample.

3. Review the steps with the students. Point out the importance of being *exact* when explaining a process. Further, explain that when someone *writes* a process, this is called *expository writing*.

4. Distribute the handout. Pair the students to explain to each other the "how to" they have selected. Allow 30 minutes for writing separately. Students will then return to their partners to read their work to each other for peer review.

Make a PB and J
s t u d e n t   h a n d o u t

You and your classmates have just instructed your teacher through the process of making a peanut butter and jelly sandwich. If you were to write this step-by-step procedure, you would be practicing *expository writing*.

Now, choose a topic. Explain how to do something so clearly that your reader will think, "That's easy. I can do that!" Here are some suggestions, but you may choose a different subject if you wish.

♦ How to Make a PB & J Sandwich
♦ How to Cook an Egg
♦ How to Ride a Bicycle
♦ How to Eat with Chopsticks
♦ How to Fly a Kite
♦ How to Plant a Tree
♦ How to Build a Snowman
♦ How to Wash Your Face

Unit 9 ♦ Queen and King for a Day
teacher's page

Objective: Students will practice *expository writing* as they provide step-by-step instructions for someone taking over their routine duties for one day.

Steps:

1.   Ask the class to participate in a fanciful situation. They are to imagine that they have won first prize in a contest. The prize is a one-day trip to any city they desire, all expenses paid, plus $1,000 to spend. The prize is for one person, so they will travel alone. They will leave at 7:00 a.m. and return at 7:00 p.m.

2.   Pair the students to talk about their destinations and their plans. Give them 10-15 minutes to do this. Invite a few students to talk about their decisions.

3.   Next, remind them that they cannot just go away without making arrangements for someone to take over their job and their duties at home. The prize committee will provide a professional to substitute for them, but this person must have detailed, step-by-step instructions to follow.

4.   Tell the students that when someone writes a plan, or a *process,* this is called *expository writing.*

5.   Give the students the handout; they will follow the instructions.

Queen and King for a Day

You have learned in this lesson that one purpose of *expository* writing is to explain how to do something. Certain words, called *transition words,* help to lead a reader step by step through the process. Some of these are: *first, second, third, after that, later on, then, next,* and *finally.*

Now, you will write a paper to explain to someone what that person needs to do to take your place tomorrow from 7:00 a.m. until 7:00 p.m. in the evening. As you write, be detailed and clear about what you expect. Think of it as a "recipe" for your day. Don't forget to use *transition words!*

Your Different Day

Tomorrow will be your different day, and I hope you enjoy it. I need you to come to my house at 6:30 in the morning because I have to leave my home at 6:45. My plane leaves at 7:30 a.m.

First, you'll make my bed. Then, you'll open the window, and make sure that my bedroom is organized. Your day will be started. My young son has school. You will have to wake him at 7:40 and take care of him because he needs your help to wash his face and brush his teeth and get dressed too. After you are done with his breakfast, you'll drive him to his school, and you will go to ESL school. There you will have a great time with the teachers. You will be at school until 12:20.

After that you'll go home and have salad for lunch, and later you'll clean the house and take care of the clothes. Then you can relax...Finally, you'll cook dinner for the whole family. After that, I'm coming home. Thank you very much.

*Rosangela, **Brazil***
(former ESL student)

Unit 10 ♦ Tick, Tock, I'm a Clock
teacher's page

Objective: Students will put themselves into the persona of a clock and write creatively about their activities and feelings.

Steps:

1. Tell students that this lesson will focus on something that people use every day: clocks. See how many clocks they can name: grandfather clocks, alarm clocks, desktop clocks, schoolhouse clocks, shelf clocks, railroad station clocks, town square clocks, travel clocks. (For this exercise, don't include watches, cellphone clocks, or computer clocks.) List the clocks they name on the board.

2. Look together at the clock on the classroom wall. Invite the class to *think as that clock*. What might they see and hear, think about and *feel*? Then, ask how many students rely on alarm clocks to waken them? Most people do not look forward to the voice of that little clock! But do they ever consider how that clock might feel?

3. Ask students to choose a clock. They will take the point of view of their clock and personify it. Pair students to talk together about their choices before writing.

4. Distribute the handout. Students will follow the directions on it.

Tick, Tock, I'm a Clock
student handout

It is time for you to write as if you were a clock for one day. Here are some questions you might ask yourself:

☞ How long has my owner had me?
☞ What do I see, hear, smell, feel around me?
☞ Is my life happy or miserable, hectic or peaceful?

Share your ideas with a partner before you begin writing.

The Grandfather Clock

When the sunlight comes through the windows, it starts a new day. I have been standing here over fifty years. Long ago a girl found me at the antique shop, and then her father bought me for her birthday. She was fifteen years old.

She and her family loved antiques. They had many antiques in their house. So I could have many friends in the house: old furniture, dolls, and dishes. I was glad to be a member of the house. Not only my friends but also she and her family greeted me. Sometimes they laughed around me and cried around me.

When she married, I was moved to a different house with some of my friends. The house was very new, so it was not comfortable for me, but I was still happy. I worked very hard, and her new husband greeted me every day.

Now she has lost her husband, and her children have their own families. She always talks to me about her memories. I listen to the stories and sometimes feel sad because we both are growing old. But I love my job. So I will continue to work for her forever.

*Akiko, **Japan***
(former ESL student)

Unit 11 ◆ Go Ahead, Exaggerate!
teacher's page

Objective: Students will add *hyperbole* to their writing skills and will demonstrate that they can use it effectively.

Steps:

1. Ask the students to define "exaggerate." (To exaggerate is to make something larger, greater, better, or worse than it is.) When do people exaggerate? (A fisherman's prize fish grows bigger and bigger at each reporting! Children also exaggerate.)

2. Explain that exaggeration in writing is called *hyperbole*. Give some English expressions containing exaggeration, and then invite the students to share some from their language:

    ◆ "It's so hot today you could fry an egg on the sidewalk!"
    ◆ "I'm so hungry I could eat a horse!"
    ◆ "That man is a moose!"
    ◆ "I'm so happy I could burst!"

3. Ask if anyone can recall a folktale or a hero story that exaggerates facts. Ask for a volunteer or two to share.

4. Distribute the handout, and follow directions on it.

Go Ahead, Exaggerate!

You learned about exaggeration, or *hyperbole,* in this class. For example, a fish often becomes larger each time a fisherman tells about catching it! Here is part of a legend about John Henry, an American hero, who died working on constructing the Chesapeake & Ohio Railroad many years ago.

> When John Henry was born, birds came from everywhere to see him. The bears and panthers and moose and deer and rabbits and squirrels and even a unicorn came out of the woods to see him. And instead of the sun tending to business and going to bed, it was peeping out from behind the moon's skirts trying to get a glimpse of the new baby.
>
> from *John Henry* by Julius Lester

Your task is to write a story that contains hyperbole. You may re-tell a story from your culture, or you may make one up. Please tell a partner your story before you write.

Unit 12 ♦ Shoes
teacher's page

Objective: Applying their understanding of *personification*, students will write how *shoes* might think and feel as they go through one day.

Materials: Catalog pictures of various kinds of footwear, such as high heels, men's dress shoes, athletic shoes, ballet slippers, cowboy boots, hiking boots, saddle shoes, loafers, Crocs

Steps:

1. Remind the class that *personification* is giving life and human characteristics to an object or an animal. In Walt Disney's **Fantasia**, for example, brooms march as they continue picking up buckets of water. In **Cinderella**, mice talk and act like humans.

2. Show the shoe pictures you have brought, and ask students to identify the kinds of shoes. Spell these on the board, as needed. Then invite the students to choose a pair to personify. They will focus on one day. To illustrate, take two or three of the pictures, and ask the class where these shoes might *go*, and what they might *see* and *do*.

3. Pair the students to talk about their choices. Circulate around the room to offer ideas if asked.

4. Read the handout, and then allow 30 minutes of writing time.

Shoes

I'm a Loafer, and He's a Loafer, Too

"Hurry up!" his mother says every morning. It's so messy in his room, so everyone calls HIM a loafer! He puts on a t-shirt and jeans. Then he picks me up and wears me, his "loafers," and quickly runs to school.

He wears me rudely and never watches out for situations on his way to school. Some-times I am washed by the water of a hole. Sometimes I eat gum somebody has chewed. That's sickening for me!

He thinks of me as all-purpose shoes. I can run even though I'm not running shoes. I can jump even though I am afraid of heights.

I am tossed under a bed when he wishes. Dark night is coming, but I can't sleep because day will come soon. It will be a nightmare again!

Michael, *Taiwan*
(former ESL student)

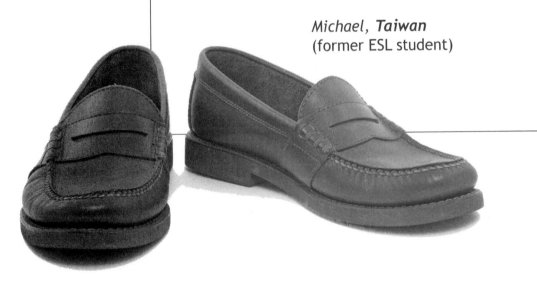

We have talked about the many types of shoes. You have selected a pair and exchanged ideas with a classmate about your choice. Write a composition as if you *are* that pair of shoes for one day, as Michael did above.

Unit 13 ◆ Attitude through Adjectives
teacher's page

Objective: Students will describe a place, and learn the strength of adjectives
            to convey feelings.

Steps:

1. Tell students that the description of an interior space will be their writing assignment
    during this class. When they write this description, they should not just objectively make
    a list of objects and their locations in the room, but they should also use *adjectives* to
    convey their feelings about where they are.

2. As a warm-up, the class could practice by describing the classroom from the viewpoint
    of the teacher, giving it a positive slant. Then students could describe the classroom
    from the viewpoint of a bored student. (As students do this, write the adjectives they use
    on the board.)

3. Distribute the handout. Students will write two spatial descriptions from two different
    viewpoints.

Attitude through Adjectives
student handout

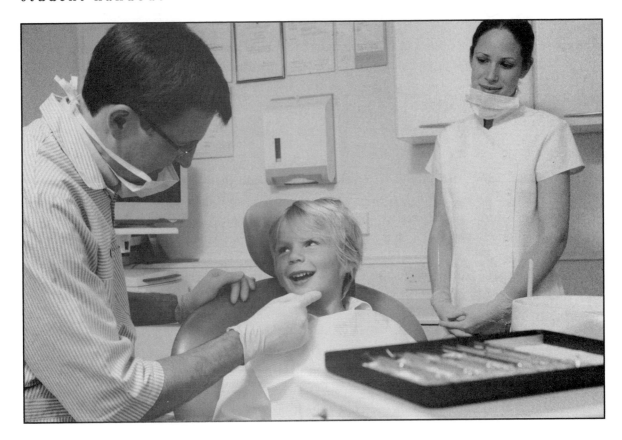

Above is a photo of a dentist and a patient in the dentist's office. Imagine that you are in that room, and write two paragraphs to *describe the room*.

In the first paragraph, imagine that you are the dentist, and write a description of the room.

In the second paragraph, imagine that you are the patient, and write a description of the room as you look at it while you are sitting in the dentist's chair.

Think about how each person feels about being in the room, and use adjectives to show your feelings.

Unit 14 ◆ An Autumn Leaf
teacher's page

Objective: Taking the "point of view" of an oak leaf, students will *feel, see, hear, smell,* and *think* as a leaf, and create a story about their life on an autumn day.

Materials: A few oak leaves

Steps:

1. Write the words "point of view" on the board. Explain that writers use point of view (also called *personification*) to write, not as themselves, but as an object or an animal. They give human characteristics to that object or animal. (Think of Mickey Mouse, for example.) They find it challenging – and fun – to "step outside" themselves to write.

2. Distribute the oak leaves. Ask students to imagine themselves as an oak leaf on an autumn day, ready to fly away from their tree.

   ◆ How might they *feel*? (Excited? Afraid? Anxious?)
   ◆ What might they *see* from their tree? *Hear*? *Smell*? *Think about*?
   ◆ Write responses on the board as students share ideas.

3. Remind the students that they should write in first person. (*I* see people walking below *me*. *I* feel the wind.)

4. Distribute the handout; read it together.

An Autumn Leaf
student handout

> *How does the wind walk?*
>
> *The wind walks in a rush*
> *brushing colored leaves*
> *from the trees as she passes.*
>
> *The wind walks in a whirl,*
> *twirling the leaves*
> *around and around*
> *before she waltzes them down streets*
> *and scatters them in faraway places.*

This passage, from *How Does the Wind Walk?* by Nancy White Carlstrom, illustrates "point of view," or *personification*. The wind is a "she" who "walks in a rush" and "twirls the leaves…before she waltzes them down streets…"

Imagine you *are* a leaf on a tall oak tree. It is a windy autumn day, and you know that you will leave your tree at any moment. Here are some questions to consider before you begin to write:

♦ *Where* are you? In the middle of a city? In a deep forest? Beside a quiet stream? Next to a noisy playground?

♦ (Use some of the five senses, as we did in class.) What do you *see*, etc.?

♦ You have experienced many kinds of weather since the spring, when you first appeared. How have you felt about these changes?

♦ Do you *want* to be blown from the tree, or do you hope to hang on?

V. Writing Activities for Pairs and Groups

Unit 1 ♦ The Personal Interview
teacher's page

Objective: Students will experience the processes of conducting and receiving a personal interview and will follow up with a written report.

Steps:

1.   This lesson works well as a get-acquainted activity for a class at the beginning of a school term. Pair students, making sure that pairs speak different first languages.

2.   Write *interview* on the board, and ask students to define it. This word has two meanings:
       a. A conversation between a news, TV, or radio personality and a famous person.
       b. A meeting between a boss and a person looking for work, to see if that person is right for the job.
     The students, practicing the first type of interview, will get to know each other by asking questions about each other's life.

3.   Distribute the handout, and review it. Explain that you will allow about 15 minutes for each interview. Stop the class after 15 minutes, and instruct students to switch roles. Then, plan about 30 minutes for the write-ups.

The Personal Interview
student handout

The Personal Interview

1. What country are you from?

2. Tell me about your family: parents, siblings.

3. Are you married?
(Or, do you have a special person in your life?)

4. Did you work in your country, or do you work now? Tell me about your job(s).

5. Do you have any special talent, hobby, or interest? Tell me why this ability is so satisfying to you.

6. What is the most unusual thing you have ever done in your life? Or, what is the most exciting place you have ever visited?

7. Finally, please tell me one unusual thing that you can say about yourself that no one else in this room can say.

Once you have finished interviewing and being interviewed, it is time to write about your partner. Start with such an entertaining introduction that your reader will wish to learn more. Then include wonderful details in the main part of your paper. Last, write a good ending. As you write, think what you can do to make your paper as unique as the person you spoke with.

Unit 2 ♦ Who Are They? What Do They Do?
teacher's page

Objective: Students will expand their understanding of a biography through cooperatvely developing a fictional life story. They will use logical organization, and they will write in past, present, and future tenses.

Materials: Magazine photos of all types of individual people

Steps:

1. Briefly relate the story of someone's life – a famous person or an interesting person. When finished, explain that an account of a life is a *biography*. Write this word on the board.

2. Pair the students, and have them tell each other about their lives – or about the life of a relative or friend. Allow 15-20 minutes.

3. Tell the students that for this activity, they will "make up" a life story. Spread the magazine pictures on a table, and have the pairs choose one for their writing focus.

4. Distribute the handout. First, gather opinions on this young woman's occupation. Then, following the handout instructions, the students will concoct their biographies.

Who Are They? What Do They Do?

student handout

What does this person do? Is she a teacher? A lawyer? A dancer? A model? An astronaut maybe? OR is she a bank robber? OR a thief who sometimes dresses all in black and sneaks into museums after dark to steal priceless art?

What is your guess?

Just now, you decided on a "profession" for this young woman. Generally, a biography is based on a real life. For this writing assignment, however, you and a classmate will now create an *imaginary* life from a photograph of a person. This life can be as exciting and adventuresome as you wish. Here are some details you may include:

- ☞ the person's name
- ☞ birthplace
- ☞ childhood (including family members)
- ☞ education
- ☞ love life
- ☞ career
- ☞ family now
- ☞ plans for the future

Unit 3 ◆ What Happens Next?
teacher's page

Objective: Students will work with a partner to produce an imaginative story.

Steps:

1. Begin to tell a story which has potential for creative development. Stop after establishing the background of the story, and elicit possible endings from the class.

2. Divide the students into pairs. Tell them they will complete a story together.

3. Distribute the student handout to each pair, and set the students to work.

What Happens Next?
student handout

Below are four story beginnings. You and your partner will choose one and will complete the story.

1. The phone rang several times Saturday night, but every time I answered it, no one spoke. I could hear soft music in the background, so I knew someone was on the other end of the phone.

2. When we moved to _____, we knew that we wanted to live in a big old house. We spent months looking for just the right one, and we thought we had found it. It has been one month since we moved into this house, but we could never have imagined all the strange things that would happen.

3. Our family decided to take a very special vacation together. We planned it for months in advance because we wanted everything to be perfect. Well, it was not perfect. This is where we went and what happened.

4. I was at home waiting for my friend to pick me up to go to a movie. I heard a noise in front of the house, and thinking it was my friend, I went to open the door. But what I saw changed my plans completely.

Unit 4 ♦ Story from a Wordless Picture Book
teacher's page

Objective: Students will see the value of choosing their words carefully as they create a story from a wordless picture book.

Materials: One children's picture book with words, such as *When the Relatives Came* or *When I Was Young in the Mountains*, both by Cynthia Rylant
Also, several wordless picture books from the library

Steps:

1. Write "picture books" on the board. Parents read these books to their children. Adults love them too for their good stories and luminous illustrations. Sometimes college writing teachers use them as models of careful wording.

2. Explain that because these books are short, authors select their words carefully. Read a Rylant book (or any you particularly like) to the class as an example.

3. In some cases, these books are "wordless," with very few – or even no – words. Show the ones you brought.

4. Then, divide students into groups of three. Let each group choose a wordless book. Go to the student handout; students will follow directions at the bottom.

Suggested titles, Wordless Picture Books

The Lion & the Mouse by Jerry Pinkney *
The Bored Book by David Michael Slater
Good Dog, Carl (or any Carl books) by Alexandra Day *
Yellow Ball by Molly Bang *
The Ring by Lisa Maizlish *
The Gray Lady and the Strawberry Snatcher by Molly Bang
Tuesday by David Wiesner *
The Story of a Little Mouse Trapped in a Book by Monique Felix *
The Plane or *The House* or *The Boat* (all by Monique Felix) *
Sidewalk Circus by Paul Fleischman and Kevin Hawkes
Mouse Around by Pat Schories
Where's My Monkey? by Dieter Schubert

Especially recommended

Story from a Wordless Picture Book
student handout

In this lesson, we discussed children's picture books. We also talked about the value of thinking about each word as you write. With your group, you have picked a wordless book from those your teacher brought to class.

Assignment:

☞ First, *tell* a story together as you go through your book.

☞ Then, study the book again, as you *write* your story. Remember to *choose your words carefully.*

☞ Read your story out loud. Eliminate any unnecessary words until you feel your writing is "just right."

Unit 5 ♦ Love Story
t e a c h e r ' s   p a g e

Objective: Students will work together to produce a narrative essay.

Materials: Pictures of people – half of men, half of women

Steps:

1. Distribute the handout. Then give each student a picture. Jotting down quick notes, the students are to create a biography for the person in the picture, supplying the information listed on the student handout. Allow students 10 to 15 minutes to create the biographies.

2. Students will take turns introducing their character to the class, being sure to include all information on the handout.

3. After the introductions are completed, pair the students by means of a raffle. Put the 'names' (which students have assigned to their pictures) of the male picture-people on slips of paper, and have each student with a female picture draw a name. Tell the pairs they will write a love story about their picture people. Using the list at the bottom of the handout as a guide, instruct the students to compose a 'love story.'

4. If time permits, the students can read their stories to the class.

Love Story
student handout

Name:

From:

Age:

Education:

Job:

Hobbies/Activities:

Where this person lives now:

In your story, include the following facts:

How these two people met
Why they liked each other
If they married
If they broke up
Their family life (children, pets)
What they are doing today

Unit 6 ♦ Writing as a Process
teacher's page

Objective: By taking part in four steps of a writing process, students will discover that good writing is a work in progress.

Materials: A small bell. Also a grab bag of everyday items, such as a spoon, a pencil, a pen, a pocketknife, a book of matches, a cloth handkerchief, a bandanna, a paperclip, a Q-tip.

Steps:

1. Ask students to define "process." Then explain that writers often follow a *process* (a step-by-step plan) as they work. Write the following on the board, clarifying each one.

    ♦ Pre-writing (brainstorming)
    ♦ First Draft
    ♦ Second Draft (*Several drafts* generally follow!)
    ♦ Editing/Revising

2. Divide students into pairs or groups of three, depending on the size of the class. Ask someone from each pair or group to take an object from your bag.

3. Go to the handout; discuss it. Depending on the object they have taken, the groups will title their papers, *The Uses of a* _____ . Working through steps one to four listed on the handout, each group will complete *one paragraph*. Allow 15 minutes for each step, ringing your bell to signal time for the next one.

4. At the end, ask someone from each group read the final version. Or type up the papers, and post them the following day.

Writing as a Process
student handout

Your teacher reminded you that writing is a *process*. Now with your partner (or group), you will practice **four important steps** in the writing process. Title your paper

The Uses of a _____.

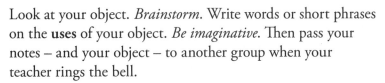

Step One: Pre-writing

Look at your object. *Brainstorm*. Write words or short phrases on the **uses** of your object. *Be imaginative*. Then pass your notes – and your object – to another group when your teacher rings the bell.

Step Two: First Draft

Take the brainstorming notes and the new object from another group. Choose the ideas you like and work them into sentences for a *first draft*. When you hear the bell, pass your paper (first draft) and the object to another group.

Step Three: Second Draft

Look at the first draft and the object you have received. Talk about how to improve the writing. Then *re-write* the sentences into a paragraph, making sure the ideas "flow" from one to another. At the bell, pass the second draft and the object to another group one last time.

Step Four: Edit/Revise

Study the second draft along with the object. Correct any spelling or grammar mistakes. Decide which sentences to keep; move a sentence to another place, perhaps. This will be the last step. Read your paragraph out loud.

Unit 7 ♦ Writing a Thank-You Note
teacher's page

Objective: Students will identify situations which call for a written response and will then compose a thank-you note.

Materials: Sample thank-you notes *(optional)*

Steps:

1. Ask the students what they might do – besides saying "thank you" – when someone does something nice for them or gives them a gift.

2. Then ask them if writing thank-you notes is a common practice in their families. Under what circumstances would a thank-you note be appropriate? How formal should it be? Can a thank-you note be creative?

3. *(Optional)* Read some sample thank-you notes you have brought with you, and invite the class's reaction to each one.

4. Distribute the handout; follow the directions indicated. Pair students to complete the writing assignment. At the conclusion of this activity, ask several pairs to share their notes.

Writing a Thank-You Note
student handout

In many circumstances, you may want to express your thanks to someone in writing. With your classmates, read the following situations, and choose the ones where you feel a thank-you note would be appropriate. Then, with your partner, select one and compose a note together.

☞ A student brought candy to class to share with everyone.

☞ Aunt Tilda gave you a beautiful red sweater for your birthday. You love it.

☞ Uncle Fred sent you a ghastly orange sweater. You **don't** like it.

☞ You were in the hospital for four days. A friend sent you flowers and a card.

☞ You were absent from school for three days. A classmate called to see how you were.

☞ Your son's teacher, Mr. Shaw, stayed after school every day last week to give him extra help with his calculus.

☞ You paid your neighbor's son to water your flowers while you were away on vacation. He did a great job.

☞ Your son's English teacher gave him an A at midterm.

☞ For your birthday, your mother-in-law sent you a check for $50.00.

☞ Your wife gave you a new shirt for your birthday.

☞ Your daughter was hit by a bicycle in front of Mr. Mascari's grocery store. Mr. Mascari called for an ambulance and stayed with your daughter until it arrived.

☞ You have just returned from a job interview, where you were told you would hear from the company in two weeks.

Unit 8 ◆ Keep Your Reader at the End of Your Pencil
teacher's page

Objective: Keeping the reader in mind, students will create two compositions on the same subject, targeting two different audiences.

Steps:

1. Ask students to define the word *audience.* (An audience is usually a group of people who watch a movie or listen to a lecture.) Do writers have an audience? If so, who are they? (*Audiences* for writers are *readers!*)

2. How should writing differ for different "audiences"? For example, ask students how words used by a children's book author would be different from those by a mystery novelist – or by a science textbook writer – or by a person applying for a job?

3. Talk about **tone** (warm, friendly, businesslike, academic), **style** (simple, rich, compelling, sophisticated), and **degree of formality**.

4. Pair students. First, ask them to choose *one* of three subjects: a **tree**, a **snake**, or a **pond**.

5. Now go to the handout; read it together. Students will address two different audiences for this assignment.

Keep Your Reader at the End of Your Pencil
student handout

In this lesson, we talked about "audience," meaning the person or people you are writing for. Keep your reader as close as the end of your pencil. Choose your words, sentence structure, tone, and organization according to who will read your work. Ask yourself, "Does my language match my reader, or is it too difficult – or too simple?"

Below are two student examples on the same topic. The first version is for a child, the second for an adult.

The Tree (Reader = child)

The maple is a beautiful tree. It likes to change its color in different seasons. It will wear light green clothes in spring. In summer, it changes to a heavy green coat. It will change to colorful dresses including red, yellow, and orange in the fall. When winter is coming, it will wear a white jacket because snow is falling. The maple tree is a magic tree because it likes to make itself up for the changing weather.

Jackie, Taiwan

The Tree (Reader = adult)

Fall is my favorite season in the U.S.
Various colors of the leaves
    Bring me into the world of poems.

Life is like the fate of the leaves.
It, too, grows, greens, dries, and falls.

May everyone catch the moments
And cherish them.

Yi-chan, Taiwan

Your assignment:

You and your partner have chosen one of three subjects: a **tree**, a **snake**, or a **pond**. **Write two separate paragraphs (or poems)**, one for a nine-year-old, the other for an adult. You may work together on both. Or, giving each other ideas, one of you can write the *child's version*, the other the *adult version*.

VI. Writing Poetry

Unit 1 ♦ A First Look at Poetry
teacher's page

Objective: After talking about what a poem "looks like," students will create two poems, one basic, the other filled with imagination.

Materials: A few simple poems*

Steps:

1.   Using a visual presenter (or document camera), show the poems you brought and read them to the class. Ask the students to tell you what a poem "looks like," as compared to the text in a book.

2.   Since writing a poem may seem intimidating to some students, pair the students, and tell them that you are going to guide them through an easy exercise.

3.   Distribute the handout. For Section 1, the pairs will list tasks they **must** do each day, such as: get dressed, eat breakfast, drive to school. (The seven activities should be in sequence.) Allow about 15 minutes. Call for volunteers to read their lists out loud.

4.   Next, working on Section 2, the pairs will use their imaginations. What can they do that has nothing to do with their everyday activities, such as: smell a flower, study a snowflake, listen to the rain? (Be **very** sparse with your ideas. See what the students come up with!)

5.   Give the class 30 minutes to complete Section 2. Last, ask several pairs to read their poems to the class.

* Here are some poems to consider:

   The Fly by Ogden Nash
   Fog by Carl Sandburg
   April Rain Song by Langston Hughes
   Who Has Seen the Wind? by Christina Rossetti
   This is Just to Say and *The Red Wheelbarrow*, both by William Carlos Williams

You can find these poems easily by typing the titles and "poem" into a Google search.

A First Look at Poetry

Section I: Every day, I remember to:

_____

_____

_____

_____

_____

_____

I don't forget!

Section II: Tomorrow, I will remember to:

_____

_____

_____

_____

_____

_____

I won't forget!

Unit 2 ♦ What's Hanging on My Clothesline?

teacher's page

Objective: After learning vocabulary words for clothing, students will finish a simple poem to reinforce these words.

Materials: Clothes, such as pants, a skirt, a blouse, a tee-shirt, pajamas, underwear, socks, etc., collected from home in a paper sack. (Or use picture dictionaries, if available.)

Steps:

1. Using your paper sack filled with clothes, take one item out at a time, identifying each. Have students pronounce the words after you. Repeat this process several times, alternating the order, until you feel that the students have mastered these words.

2. Then, add the following words:

   ☞ clothesline
   ☞ laundry
   ☞ strong winds

3. Pair the students, and give each pair the handout. Instruct the pairs to choose the items on their clothesline, using the new vocabulary. For fun, they might add, "Aunt Po's pajamas" or "Grandfather's underwear." In the second part, they will repeat the original items. Inform the students at the end that they just completed a poem!

The Clothesline

A sunny day, and laundry's fun!

_____ hanging on my clothesline
_____ hanging on my clothesline
_____ hanging on my clothesline
_____ hanging on my clothesline
_____ hanging on my clothesline
_____ hanging on my clothesline
_____ hanging on my clothesline

Clothes all dance beneath the sun!

Weather changes, strong winds blow

_____ flying off my clothesline
_____ flying off my clothesline
_____ flying off my clothesline
_____ flying off my clothesline
_____ flying off my clothesline
_____ flying off my clothesline
_____ flying off my clothesline!

Where they go, I'll never know!

Unit 3 ♦ Another Look at Poetry
teacher's page

Objective: Working as a class first, and then in pairs (or individually), students will create poetry.

Materials: Selected poems, enlarged and perhaps laminated

Steps:

1. Tell the students that poets are artists, but instead of oils or watercolors, they use *words* to *paint pictures*. Some poems are short; others are long. Some poems rhyme; others do not.

2. Poets write about *emotions*: joy, sadness, fear, hope, love, grief, melancholy. Show the poems you brought, using a visual presenter or document camera, and read them to the class. Be sure the students notice the *look* of a poem, as different from that of prose.

3. Invite the students to write a class poem, using the following steps:

    ♦ Call on a student to name his or her favorite color. Write it on the board.
    ♦ Ask another student to think of two adjectives describing that color. Write them on the board.
    ♦ Choose a third student to decide on three things with that color. Write them on the board.
    ♦ End the poem with "(The color) makes me feel _____."
    (See an example on the student handout.)

4. Now, ask students to each choose their favorite color and write a poem similar to the class poem. When finished, pair students to read to each other. Ask three or four to read theirs to the class.

5. Distribute the handout. Students will follow directions at the bottom.

Another Look at Poetry
student handout

pink

pink
warm, tender
doll, dream, passion

pink
  makes me feel
      that I am a girl in love.

*Ching, **Taiwan***
(former ESL student)

Autumn

Someone knocked at my door
When I was dozing
On a gorgeous autumn day
All red and yellow and orange

No one knocked at the door!
My old tree
Had dropped its chestnuts

On the gutter of the roof…
Hundreds of chestnuts from the tree
Millions of chestnuts over the grass
Chestnuts singing on my roof

Knocking on the roof
Again and again
They let me know winter will come
                soon
Thank you, my chestnuts
And thank you,
                my favorite season

*Yukiko, **Japan***
(former ESL student)

In this class, you wrote a class poem, and you wrote your own poem. Now it is time for you to write another poem. You may work with another person, or you may work alone.

You will write about:

♦ One of the seasons **or**
♦ A phenomenon of nature
  (rain, snow, hail, thunder, fog, sunshine, a sunset, a sunrise…)

Unit 4 ♦ Poetry and Rhyme
teacher's page

Objective: Students will understand how rhyme is used in poetry and will create a
              poem using a rhyme scheme.

Steps:

1. Write the poem "Twinkle, Twinkle, Little Star" on the board and underline the last word
    in each line.

        Twinkle, twinkle little star
        How I wonder what you are,
        Up above the world so high
        Like a diamond in the sky.

    Ask students if they see anything special about the underlined words. If they cannot
    decipher the pattern, write "a, a, b, b" to indicate the rhyming pattern. If they still cannot
    see the pattern, tell them that the words you underline *rhyme*. Point out how *star* and *are*
    and *high* and *sky* rhyme, and how the pattern is arranged.

2. Write the rhyme "Pease Porridge Hot" on the board and ask students what the rhyming
    pattern for this poem is (a, b, a, b):

        Pease porridge hot,
        Pease porridge cold,
        Pease porridge in the pot
        Nine days old!

    Talk about how rhyme in English is based on sound and not on spelling. (*Star* and *are*
    rhyme and the word endings are spelled almost the same. Words like *late* and *eight* and
    two and *shoe* rhyme not because of the spelling of the words but because of the sounds
    of the syllables.

    Tell the students that when we think of poems in English, we often think of rhyming
    words at the end of each phrase. There are many short poems that rhyme, but there
    are also some longer poems that rhyme, such as the poem on the student handout.

3. Pair the students and distribute the handout. Have them look for the words that rhyme.
    Also, have them label the rhyme pattern.

4. Instruct the pairs to follow the directions at the bottom of the sheet to write a short
    rhyming poem of their own.

Poetry and Rhyme
student handout

The Arrow and the Song

I shot an arrow into the air,
It fell to earth, I knew not where;
For, so swiftly it flew, the sight
Could not follow it in its flight.

I breathed a song into the air,
It fell to earth, I knew not where;
For who has sight so keen and strong,
That it can follow the flight of song?

Long, long afterward, in an oak
I found the arrow, still unbroke;
And the song, from beginning to end,
I found again in the heart of a friend.

by Henry Wadsworth Longfellow

Label the rhyming pattern for this poem. Can you hear the musical characteristics?

Using one of the rhyme patterns we talked about, write a poem with your partner.

Unit 5 ♦ Color Your Poem
teacher's page

Objective: Choosing a color, students will "define" it in a poem saturated with vivid vocabulary words. (This unit expands on a "color" idea in an earlier unit, Another Look at Poetry.)

Materials: A copy of either *Hailstones and Halibut Bones* by Mary O'Neill or *Dream* by Susan Bosak. Also, color swatches from a paint store.

Steps:

1. Invite students to name their favorite color, and to explain their feelings about that color. Then, read a sample or two from either of the books above.

2. Let each student choose one of the color swatches you brought. Pair students to brainstorm ideas as they define their colors. For example, what is red? If they begin, "Red is…" how might they continue? What objects and/or feelings come to mind? They should select their words carefully.

3. After 15 minutes, have some pairs share their insights.

4. Distribute the handout. Using the sample poems as guides—and the color swatches— instruct each student to paint a color poem in words. Students will need to "stretch" their vocabulary. They should avoid overused, "colorless" words such as *happy*, *bad*, *good*, and *nice*.

This unit was adapted from a lesson by Bernie Mossotti, author and teacher of "Poetry in Motion," Center for Creative Learning, Rockwood School District, St. Louis, Missouri.

Color Your Poem
s t u d e n t   h a n d o u t

Gray

Gray is the cold
Gray is the sad wolf's call
Gray is the wind running up your spine
Gray is the squirrel
Scurrying up and down trees
Gray is the shell of an old turtle
Gray is dead leaves

Elise
(Center for Creative Learning Student)

Pearl White

White is a dove on a wedding day
the bride's dress
a cold bed to rest your head
crystal white sand
popcorn without butter
a piece of paper blank to the bone
socks on your feet to keep them warm
a never-used napkin
a light bulb turned off
the dance of a snowflake on a winter's day
a necklace of pearls
White is not plain
cream is white's younger sister—
for if no white—no cream!
Angel white

Haley
(Center for Creative Learning Student)

Unit 5 ♦ Put Yourself in Poetry
teacher's page

Objective: Stepping outside of themselves, students will think as a tree as they create poetry.

Materials: Photographs from Google Images of different species of trees, copied and posted around the room

Steps:

1. See if students can define personification. (Personification gives a voice and human characteristics to a non-speaking thing or animal.)

2. Now ask the students to think about an experience they have had with a tree. Did they ever climb a tree and look down on the world? Did they have a swing attached to a tree branch? Did they pick fruit from a tree? Did they hide behind a tree?

3. Encourage them to think about trees in a new way. What might a tree see…hear… smell…feel…imagine…understand…fear…wish for…dream about…whisper … remember…love? Gather responses on a visual presenter or document camera. Can anyone see a poem emerging?

4. Go to the handout; read the poems together out loud. Finally, students will think as a tree as they create their poems.

This unit was adapted from a lesson by Bernie Mossotti, author and teacher of "Poetry in Motion," Center for Creative Learning, Rockwood School District, St. Louis, Missouri.

Put Yourself in Poetry

student handout

I am a tree that lets birds lay their eggs
I am a tree that lets foxes snuggle
I am a tree that has hives for bees
I am a tree that lets owls in
I am a tree that lets butterflies light on me
I am a tree that lets bark beetles in
I am a tree who is a playground for children
I am a tree who has visitors picnic.

Jared
(Center for Creative Learning student)

so still I stand—
my leaves rust,
summer worn and wind weary
so still the cool air
refreshing
it reminds me that soon
winter white will wrap me
snug tight
I will sleep
and dream of bursting life

Bernie Mossotti

Now, imagine that you are a tree.
Think about your life as that tree as you develop your poem.

Appendix

Handouts for
III. Writing Around
the Holidays

Valentine's Day

How did Valentine's Day begin? Legends tell of wolves wandering the fields of ancient Rome. They killed cows and sheep, and they frightened farmers and their families. The people believed that a god named Lupercus then scared the wolves away. Each February, they gave thanks to Lupercus at a festival called Lupercalia. At the festival, young women's names were dropped into a large vase. To choose a partner for the festival, young men reached into the vase to pick out a name. Frequently people fell in love during Lupercalia.

Later, a priest named Valentine got into trouble with the emperor, Claudius. Rome was at war, and Claudius commanded his soldiers think about war, not love. He stopped all marriages. Valentine continued to perform marriage ceremonies secretly. When Claudius found out, he was furious. He threw Valentine into prison and executed him on February 14th.

When all Rome became Christian, Valentine was made a saint. The church leaders remembered the old holidays, like Lupercalia, but changed their names and their meanings. Lupercalia became St. Valentine's Day, a day to celebrate love.

In the 1860s, during the Civil War in the United States, Valentine's Day became popular in this country. People continue to give each other cards, chocolate, flowers, and small gifts. Some people even write poetry—straight from their hearts—to their loves!

Unit 2 ♦ Heroes in History
s t u d e n t   h a n d o u t

George Washington

When Americans celebrate Presidents' Day on the third Monday in February, they remember two heroic presidents, George Washington and Abraham Lincoln.

They honor George Washington because he was the "father" of the country; that is, he was the first president of the United States. His portrait is on the one-dollar bill and on the quarter. In addition, the capital of the United States was named in his memory, as were many smaller cities throughout the country.

George Washington was best known for his honesty. There is a story that as a child, he chopped down a cherry tree. When his father found the tree lying on the ground, he very angrily asked George if he had cut it. George replied, "Father, I cannot tell a lie. I did it with my ax." This story has provided children a model of honesty up to the present time. We now know this story is a myth, but it continues to be told to children.

Before becoming president, George Washington was a great general in the United States' war against Great Britain to gain its independence. It was an extremely difficult job because the American troops were not comparable to Great Britain's.

Abraham Lincoln

Another hero, Abraham Lincoln, was the 16th president of the United States. He is famous because he served as president during the Civil War of the country. He also wrote the Emancipation Proclamation, which freed the slaves. Like Washington, there are cities named after him, and his portrait is on the five-dollar bill and the penny.

Lincoln is a hero because he was born in poverty, educated himself, and became a lawyer and then president of the United States. Lincoln's life provides American children with a model of someone who started with very little to become the most powerful man in his country. Children are taught that they can work hard and become whatever they want, just as Abraham Lincoln did.

(shamrocks)

St. Patrick's Day, March 17th, is an Irish holiday honoring St. Patrick. He was a missionary who many people believe converted the people of Ireland to Christianity in the 5th century A.D. The first American celebration of St. Patrick's Day was in Boston in 1737. It is not a national holiday in the United States, and schools, banks, and post offices are NOT closed.

In America, St. Patrick's Day is basically a time to wear green – shirts, socks, ties, or just a flower or ribbon. Green is associated with St. Patrick's Day because it is the color of spring, Ireland, and the shamrock. Other things we associate with this day are leprechauns (tiny men who know where a pot of gold is buried), a shillelagh (a wooden walking stick), and the saying, "Erin Go Bragh" which means "Ireland forever" in Gaelic, the national language of Ireland.

It is also a time to party. There are St. Patrick's Day parades in many cities throughout the United States on March 17th. These are organized by the Ancient Order of Hibernians, a national organization for U.S. citizens who are of Irish birth or descent. It preserves and promotes Irish art, dance, music, and sports here in America. The biggest parade this organization sponsors is the St. Patrick's Day Parade in New York City.

On St. Patrick's Day, many stores sell foods that have been colored green, such as cookies, cakes, and breads. Restaurants prepare special foods, such as corned beef and cabbage and Irish stew (lamb, onions, and potatoes). Many bars even sell green scrambled eggs and green beer.

There is a saying that on St. Patrick's Day, everyone is Irish! This means that even if people are not Irish, they can celebrate this day by wearing green and partying, and many people do. As a joke, people will refer to their "Irish" heritage by adding the letter "O" to their last names. This is because many Irish surnames begin with the letter "O," such as O'Brien, O'Toole, and O'Casey. Jokingly, some people refer to their last names as O'Suzuki, O'Garcia, and O'Pulaski!

So this St. Patrick's Day, you can join in the celebration by wearing green and eating green-colored food. You can even change your name for a day!

Turnips into Pumpkins

A very long time ago, Druids, priests from England and France, believed that ghosts of the dead came to harm people one night of every year. People feared these teachings, so they hid behind costumes and masks to keep their identity secret from the evil spirits. Also, to frighten away these spirits, people hollowed out turnips, carved scary faces into them, and put them in their windows.

In 610 A.D., the Catholic Church chose November 1st as All Saints' Day. The old Druid beliefs and the Catholic special day combined to become Halloween. Halloween means *hallowed*—or holy—evening. It always falls on October 31st, and it is celebrated in many countries around the world.

In the United States, children visit houses wearing costumes (witches, skeletons, pirates, princesses, storybook characters) and asking for candy. Some adults dress in costumes and attend parties. Halloween has become the second most-decorated holiday in America. (The first is Christmas.) Houses, malls, and stores dress in the colors of Halloween: black for dark night and orange for autumn and pumpkins. Pumpkins, carved into jack-o-lanterns and lit with candles inside, sit on front porches and in windows.

Why don't we still carve turnips as ancient people did, and where did pumpkins originate for Halloween? In North America, pumpkins were larger than turnips, easier to carve, and more available.

On a warm September day in 1620, one hundred and two people, along with two dogs and a cat, left England to sail across the ocean in search of religious freedom in a new land. They were called Pilgrims.

Their ship, the *Mayflower*, was as big as two trucks. Pilgrims and sailors crowded together to sleep and eat. Children had no room to run and no toys, as they had left most things behind. Many of the Pilgrims hated the food on the ship: salted beef and fish; hard, dry biscuits; a little cheese. After a while, the food spoiled, and there wasn't enough water for drinking and washing. Everyone slept on the hard, dry floor of the ship in the same clothes they wore every day. Their clothes became torn, dirty, and smelly.

Day by day the weather worsened. Storms came. The wind howled. The *Mayflower* shuddered as it rose and fell in seas as high as mountains. Rain drenched the ship and the Pilgrims. Most of them got sick, and many died.

After sixty-five days, they spotted land. Everyone went ashore. It was very cold, and

snowflakes danced. But the children raced up and down the beach, and women washed clothes in a shallow pond. The Pilgrims were glad, but frightened. Winter was coming, and they had to find a safe place to live. They discovered a deserted Indian village with rivers nearby and good land for planting. Quickly they set to work, building homes from tree bark and branches. At night, they slept on the *Mayflower*.

The first winter was horrible. The Pilgrims could not finish building their homes before the heavy snows came, and they could not find enough food in the forest. Almost half died that first winter. When spring came, Squanto and Samoset, two Native Americans, wandered into their village. They began teaching the Pilgrims about the land they knew well. They taught them to fish, to hunt for deer and turkeys, to plant seeds, to find wild plants – some good to eat and others to use as medicine.

By summer, seven houses were finished. Gardens were bursting with vegetables. The Pilgrims met more friendly Indians. They made flour, baked cornbread, and often ate together. By fall, the Pilgrims decided to celebrate their first year in their new country with a time of thanksgiving.

The first Thanksgiving lasted three days. The Pilgrims and Indians shared a feast of wild turkeys and geese from the forest, lobsters, clams, oysters, and fish from the waters. From the gardens, they gathered cucumbers, carrots, turnips, onions, beets, corn, and squash. Ninety Indians came. Children played games and had jumping and running contests.

Today, American families all over the United States celebrate Thanksgiving on the fourth Thursday of November to remember their ancestors.

Skills Index

Adjectives:
Attitude Through Adjectives
Section III Unit 13 ♦ page 106

Brainstorming:
Strange Encounters of a New Kind *I 22* ♦ 44
An Imaginary Trip to an Art Museum *IV 2* ♦ 84

Comparison and Contrast:
Changes *I 21* ♦ 42
Voyages and Thanksgiving *III 6* ♦ 78

Dialogue:
One More Frog and Toad *IV 7* ♦ 94

Hyperbole:
Go Ahead, Exaggerate! *IV 11* ♦ 102

Hyphenated Modifiers:
Teacher *I 6* ♦ 12

Imagery: Rain *I 24* ♦ 48
Snow *I 25* ♦ 50
Choose Your Season *I 26* ♦ 52

Mood:
Take Your Reader Shopping *I 16* ♦ 32

Narrowing Focus:
One More Frog and Toad *IV 7* ♦ 94
Your City or Town: A Detail in Focus *I 19* ♦ 38

Poetry:
See the *Writing Poetry* section, pages 130-142

Point of View:
What Am I? *IV 4* ♦ 88

Personification:
I Am A… *IV 5* ♦ 90
Tick Tock, I'm a Clock *IV 10* ♦ 100
Shoes *IV 12* ♦ 104
An Autumn Leaf *IV 14* ♦ 108

Sensory Writing:
Are You Listening? *II 1* ♦ 56
Smell and Memory *II 2* ♦ 58
Touch *II 3* ♦ 60
Spring's Here! *II 4* ♦ 62
Chocolate Chip Cookie Day *II 5* ♦ 64
An Autumn Leaf *IV 14* ♦ 108

Similes and Metaphors:
Snow *I 25* ♦ 50
Choose Your Season *I 26* ♦ 52

Speed Writing:
Memories in Small Bags *I 12* ♦ 24

Transitions:
Changes *I 21* ♦ 42
Make a PB and J *IV 8* ♦ 96
Queen and King for a Day *IV 9* ♦ 98

Writing in the Descriptive:
Mother *I 2* ♦ 4
Father *I 3* ♦ 6
What's Your Name? *I 4* ♦ 8
Teacher *I 6* ♦ 12
Best Friend *I 7* ♦ 14
First Love *I 8* ♦ 16
Cat, Dog, Parrot? *I 9* ♦ 18
Happiness *I 10* ♦ 20
Influences: People in Our Lives *I 11* ♦ 22
The Character Sketch *I 14* ♦ 28
Favorite Place *I 15* ♦ 30
Take Your Reader Shopping *I 16* ♦ 32
Mementos *I 18* ♦ 36
Your City or Town: A Detail in Focus *I 19* ♦ 38
Something from Home *I 20* ♦ 40
Conversation – A Lost Art? *I 23* ♦ 46
Writing from the Heart *III 1* ♦ 68
St. Patrick's Day *III 3* ♦ 72
Finding Beauty in the Ordinary *IV 1* ♦ 82
An Imaginary Trip to an Art Museum *IV 2* ♦ 84
Drawing Into Writing *IV 3* ♦ 86

Writing in the Expository:
Make a PB and J *IV 8* ♦ 96
Queen and King for a Day *IV 9* ♦ 98

Writing in the Narrative:
Childhood Memories *I 1* ♦ 2
What's Your Name? *I 4* ♦ 8
My First Day of School *I 5* ♦ 10
Cat, Dog, Parrot? *I 9* ♦ 18
Reflections on Water *I 13* ♦ 26
The Gift *I 17* ♦ 34
Mementos *I 18* ♦ 36
Something from Home *I 20* ♦ 40
Heroes in History *III 2* ♦ 70
St. Patrick's Day *III 3* ♦ 72
Boo! *III 4* ♦ 74
Ghost Stories *III 5* ♦ 76
Finding Beauty in the Ordinary *IV 1* ♦ 82
Drawing Into Writing *IV 3* ♦ 86
Folktales and Storytelling *IV 6* ♦ 92
One More Frog and Toad *IV 7* ♦ 94

Faces: *Characters in Search of Authors* by Patrick Moran

This is a book of 50 **photocopyable** drawings of faces ideal for use with *Section V Writing Activities for Pairs and Groups: Unit 2 Who Are They? What Do They Do?* The faces are of boys and girls, women and men; there are ten children, teens, young adults, middle aged adults, and seniors. The drawings do not reveal the person's nationality, ethnicity, or occupation; the characters could be from anywhere. This leaves students as free as possible to use their imaginations creatively. These faces can be used in the writing activity on page 114 in this book, but they can also be used in many other conversation and cultural exploration activities as suggested by Dr. Moran.

Writing Inspirations: *Over 700 Writing Topics* by Arlene Marcus

This is a collection of photocopyable cards, each with an individualized writing topic. There are 238 cards (two to a page). Most give a choice of several variations so that students can choose from over 700 different ideas to talk and then write about. Giving your students a choice stimulates motivation and creativity. There are 19 types of topics/inspirations, all illustrated, ranging in difficulty from high-beginning to high-intermediate.

♦ *Three Writing Texts* by David Kehe and Peggy Dustin Kehe ♦

Write after Input - high-beginning to intermediate

Developing Paragraphs and Compositions from Listenings and Readings
Through five units, students develop their writing skills, from learning to write a good paragraph in Unit 1 to a five-paragraph composition.

Writing Strategies - a student-centered approach to essay writing

Students follow a careful sequence of steps, from preparing first drafts to writing final essays, in *eight retorical modes*: **Book One: High-Intermediate** – presents four modes: Description, Narration, Exposition, and Comparison and Contrast. **Book Two: Advanced** - presents Process, Cause and Effect, Extended Definition, and Argumentation essays. This work is supplemented with *Fluency Writing* exercises and exercises focused on *Grammar Problems and Terminology* specially relevant to the retorical modes being taught.

♦ *Three Multi-Skills Texts* by Catherine Sadow and Judy DeFilippo ♦

Great Dictations – high-beginning to intermediate
Interactive Dictations – intermediate
Dictations for Discussion – intermediate to advanced

In each book, high-interest articles are first presented as dictations and then used as the basis for discussion, followed by writing and/or internet research.